MW00412971

THOMAS
JEFFERSON'S
FREETHOUGHT
LEGACY

THOMAS JEFFERSON'S FREETHOUGHT LEGACY

A Saying Per Day
by the
Sage of Monticello

ROGER E. GREELEY

Prometheus Books

59 John Glenn Drive
Amherst, New York 14228-2197

Published 1995 by Prometheus Books

Thomas Jefferson's Freethought Legacy: A Saying Per Day by the Sage of Monticello. Copyright © 1995 by Roger E. Greeley. All rights reserved. No part of this publication may be reproduced, stored in a retrieval system, or transmitted in any form or by any means, electronic, mechanical, photocopying, recording, or otherwise, without prior written permission of the publisher, except in the case of brief quotations embodied in critical articles and reviews. Inquiries should be addressed to Prometheus Books, 59 John Glenn Drive, Amherst, New York 14228–2197, 716–691–0133. FAX: 716–691–0137.

99 98 97 96 95   5 4 3 2 1

Library of Congress Cataloging-in-Publication Data

Jefferson, Thomas, 1743–1826.
    Thomas Jefferson's freethought legacy : a saying per day by the Sage of Monticello / Roger E. Greeley.
        p.   cm.
    Includes bibliographical references.
    ISBN 1-57392–008–8 (hardback : alk. paper)
    1. Jefferson, Thomas, 1743–1826—Views on free thought. 2. Free thought—United States. I. Greeley, Roger E. II. Title.
E302.J442   1995
973.4'6'092—dc20   95–31633
                                                                          CIP

Printed in the United States of America on acid-free paper

For Robert Merritt, an honest Jeffersonian and a good friend.

Introduction

On the occasion of Thomas Jefferson's 231st birthday, I paid
tribute to the great man in a speech delivered to a group of students. Following the talk, a number of students took exception
declaring in effect: "Your unbridled enthusiasm is inappropri-
ate. The man you call America's DaVinci was also a slave-
holding fornicator! Why did you ignore these aspects of the
man's life?" This assault was followed by another in which Jefferson was labeled a "fuzzy theist" and one who hardly qualifies
as a "major contributor to Freethought." "After all," I was told,
"remember the inscription on the Jefferson Memorial: 'I have
sworn upon the altar of *God* eternal hostility against every
form of tyranny over the mind of man,' and his direct reference
to God in the Declaration of Independence."

As I drove home that evening, it occurred to me that a
good anthology of quotes from Jefferson was needed, one that
would establish, beyond dispute, his enormous contributions to
rationalism, freethought, and science. Often, historians and
especially politicians have selected from his multivolume
legacy only those quotes that reflect conventional religiosity

7

and beliefs. In this collection great care has been exercised to exclude those quotes and present, instead, his freethought legacy. Is this bias preferable to one that selects quotes supporting a traditional religious outlook? It is my firm belief that in his *conduct of life*, Jefferson's actions were the personification of responsible freethought. (The term *freethought* came into use after Jefferson's death. It was a direct, philosophical descendant of rationalism.)

While in his writings you can find quotes endorsing the moralizing and ethics of Jesus, you cannot point to even one of his actions that might be interpreted as promoting the mainstream, organized religion of his era. He was an outspoken critic of the church and the clergy, which he often attacked with a bluntness totally uncharacteristic for a politician. Throughout his long public-service career he *never* wavered in his firm conviction of the absolute necessity for a wall of separation between church and state.

If it is by "our works we shall be known," consider Jefferson's lifelong dedication to each of the following:

1. the absolute separation of church and state.
2. the primacy of reason and science, as opposed to religious faith, superstition, or divine edicts by kings or priests.
3. the absolute need for the protections of the Bill of Rights at every level of government.
4. the desirability and inevitability of the abolition of slavery. (Upon his death his own slaves were freed.)
5. the necessity of unfettered free inquiry in science and the pursuit of truth particularly in science, which often was and still is under attack by organized religion.
6. the importance of physical fitness, which he himself observed as long as was able.
7. a loathing of monarchy and hereditary succession.
8. a limitation of government in scope and function.

Between Jefferson's presidency and that of John F. Kennedy, no equivalent spokesman on behalf of church-state separation has occupied the White House. By and large our Chief Executive reflects or toadies to the prevailing religiosity of our society. With Jefferson (and JFK) there could be no compromise on the separation of church and state. While some interpret this rigidity as being antireligious, it is well to bear in mind that religion was a private but important matter in the life of Thomas Jefferson. He even took the time to cull from the New Testament what he perceived to be the great truths of the man from Nazareth. Never, however, did he use any public office to advance his religious philosophy.

The era in which he made such significant contributions was characterized by many similarly unorthodox individuals. One example should suffice. Leo Pfeffer in *Church, State and Freedom* (Boston: Beacon Press, 1953), p. 109, makes this astonishing observation:

> It is perhaps symbolic of the difference in the relationship of state and religion between the Continental Congress and the new government established by the Constitutional Convention of 1787 [that] . . . whereas the Continental Congress instituted the practise of daily prayers immediately on first convening, the Convention met for four months without any recitation of prayers. After the Convention had been in session for a month, the octogenarian Franklin, who in earlier years had been pretty much of a Deist, moved "that henceforth prayers imploring the assistance of Heaven and its blessings on our deliberations, be held in this Assembly every morning before we proceed to business, and that one or more of the clergy of this City be requested to officiate in that service." The motion was received politely but not without embarrassment. According to the records of the Convention, "After several unsuccessful attempts for silently postponing the matter by adjourning, the adjournment was

at length carried without any vote on the motion." More than symbolic, it is deeply significant that whereas there was scarcely a document or promulgation issued by the Continental Congress that did not contain an invocation to "God" or one of the numerous synonyms of the Deity, the Constitution emerging from the convention contained no such invocation or reference.

Today, when the Religious Right demands that "we return to the religious faith of our Forefathers, the God-fearing founders of this republic," I wholeheartedly concur, providing, of course, that the "Forefathers" were those who wrote the Constitution and the Bill of Rights!

It comes as a distinct surprise to many living today to discover the true "religious makeup" of the population during the era of the Founding Fathers. At great length, Pfeffer presents a picture that is at complete variance with the portrait we were nurtured on as impressionable students K through 12. Consider this disclosure by Pfeffer:

> Exact figures do not exist on church affiliation or lack of church affiliation in the second half of the 18th century. Authorities do agree, however, that affiliation was extremely small. . . . Colonial America contained the largest proportion of unchurched in Christendom. Even in New England, the most churched section of the thirteen colonies, there was not more than one church member to every eight persons in the total population at the close of the colonial period. In respect to the population of the total country, the best estimate is that church affiliation at the founding of the republic was limited to four percent of the population. (Ibid., p. 85)

There is widespread ignorance of our actual "religious heritage." Deism was most popular for many of the Founding

Fathers. Inasmuch as traditional theists regard Deists in much the same light as atheists, the Religious Right would be revolted by the actual religious views of our forebears. If, indeed, by the standards of the "true believers" Deism, atheism, rationalism, and the absolute separation of church and state are depraved, is it not wonderful that we acquired such a fine blueprint for government considering the apostasy of its authors?

May this little volume restore your confidence in freethought, rationalism, humanism, and the importance of reason, science, and education. Jefferson was a very great voice on behalf of these eternal verities, which today are under almost constant attack from the Religious Right and their followers.

Editor's note:

I have taken the liberty of editing some of the quotes, but not in any substantive manner or out of context. Jefferson had an affection for commas that did not enhance his written expression. As the reader may know, he also wished for the adoption of phonetic spelling. This is another battle he lost along with his crusade for the adoption of the metric system in weights and measures.

Jefferson's Life: A Thumbnail Sketch

Thomas Jefferson was born April 13, 1743. He was the third child of Peter Jefferson and Jane Randolph Jefferson. His mother died March 31, 1776, just two months before Jefferson wrote the Declaration of Independence. She had borne ten children. Tom outlived all of his siblings.

He attended the college of William and Mary in Williamsburg, Virginia, graduating April 25, 1762. It would be ten years before he married Martha Wayles. Tom and Martha did not have a church wedding but instead were married at the "Forest"—her father's estate in Williamsburg. Martha was twenty-three, Thomas, twenty-nine, when they exchanged their vows. Martha bore six children, five girls and a son. Her firstborn, Martha Washington, was the only child to survive her father. Thomas Jefferson knew the pain and tragedy of burying *five* of his children as well as his wife, who died at just thirty-three years of age. (Jefferson was a widower at thirty-nine!)

Jefferson was the third president of the United States. The first two, Washington and Adams, were Federalists. Jefferson was elected as an anti-Federalist. Today his party affiliation is referred to as "Democratic-Republican." In his writings, Jefferson frequently exhalts the word "Republican," but this is not to be confused with the party of Lincoln. The present-day Republican party was founded in 1854 and attracted many members of the Whig and Free-Soil parties with some antislavery Democrats and a number of influential industrialists from the northeast. As a classical liberal, Jefferson often sounds more like a Libertarian than a Democrat or a Republican. There is no getting away from the fact that he feared and worked against a strong central government. Numerous quotes reveal his unyielding confidence in reason, education and self-reliance, and his conviction that government should be reduced to the role of policeman and arbiter, but should not become an engine for social and economic change. The reader will discover that even in 1800, Jefferson was concerned about the growth and complexity of the government he inherited from John Adams!

As to Jefferson's professed religion, no specific denomination signed him up. In the last year of his life, however, in a letter to Benjamin Waterhouse, he wrote:

> The population of my neighborhood is too slender and is too much divided into other sects to maintain any one preacher well. I must therefore be contented to a be a Unitarian by

myself although I know there are many around me who would gladly become so if once they could hear the questions fairly stated. (Letter to B. Waterhouse, Jan. 8, 1825)

Much has been made of Jefferson's great admiration for the ethics and morals of Jesus but this is to be regarded as his own *personal and private religion*. It was never to be espoused by Jefferson, directly or indirectly, while holding any public office.

Much more than his nominal acceptance of Unitarianism was his lifelong passion for the absolute separation of church and state. Again and again, Jefferson speaks of the necessity of a "wall of separation between church and state." As president (and forever after) not once did he violate his position on the absolute separation of church and state. In fact, as president he *refused* to offer a Thanksgiving proclamation. John Locke had written in his famous *Letter Concerning Toleration*, "Lastly, those are *not* at all to be tolerated who deny the being of God." Jefferson clearly departs from Locke, writing, "but where he [Locke] stopped short, we may go on."* In spite of the numberless attempts to either gloss over or deny Jefferson's total absorption in and commitment to freethought, his conduct is sufficient refutation.

These attitudes and actions earned him considerable enmity from the clergy and their devoted sheep. Writing in 1900, Dr. S. E. Forman observes:

Attacks upon him as "an atheist" and "French infidel" were also not wanting. . . . In September, 1800 a pamphlet was published in New York City by an intimate friend of Gen. Hamilton entitled, "The Voice of Warning to Christians on the Ensuing Election." It was devoted to showing that, in various particulars, Jefferson had . . . directly attacked the

*Thomas Jefferson on John Locke, *Papers of Thomas Jefferson*, vol. 1, p. 548.

authenticity of the Scriptures. . . . It retailed many stories of
Jefferson's "lack of" decent respect for the faith and worship
of Christians. Jefferson took no notice of these, save to
allude to them in a letter to Dr. Rush. He wrote that the late
attack of the Federalists on the freedom of the press "had
given to the clergy a very favorite hope of obtaining an
establishment of a particular form of Christianity throughout the United States."

It is in this letter to Dr. Rush, and in the same context, that Jefferson gives us the quote chiseled in the stone of the lovely Jefferson Memorial in Washington, D.C.: "I have sworn upon
the altar of God eternal hostility against every form of tyranny
over the mind of man."

In 1974, an able historian, Fawn Brodie, gave substantial
proof that Jefferson sired a number of children through his sex-
ual activity with a slave. A number of people have used this
news to impugn the greatness of Jefferson. That Jefferson lost
his wife when he was but thirty-nine, never remarried, but
remained sexually active should shock no one. Following the
above-mentioned memorial tribute I offered on Jefferson's
231st birthday, a college history professor challenged me by
declaring: "Have you read the new biography of Jefferson by
Fawn Brodie? If so, how come you didn't mention his five ille-
gitimate kids?"

I replied: "Why should I? Even you (or I) could do that!"
We live at a time when no public figure is allowed to have a
private life. Whatever Jefferson, Franklin Delano Roosevelt,
Margaret Sanger, or any other public person did "off stage"
truly is irrelevant and insignificant, unless the indiscretion had
a negative and governing effect on the individual's conduct of
his or her office. If we are to demand character without blemish when evaluating the great people, our list will be very short

---

Life and Writings of Thomas Jefferson (Bowen-Merrill Co., 1900), p. 80.

indeed! Prurient interest furnishes fodder for the ghoulish tabloids, but the legacy of giants is not diminished by the pygmies of the press.

The reader should note that Jefferson's devotion to civil liberties, maintaining a solid wall of separation between church and state, and his anticlericalism burned brightly in the Sage of Monticello even after celebrating his seventy-seventh birthday. The sun might be dropping in the west, but it was still on the rise in his ever-active and passionate concern for human rights. In other words, even in the late evening of his life, Thomas Jefferson was still passionately devoted to the causes for which he, along with Tom Paine, were the great champions.

Jefferson will continue to stand tall in our history because of his versatility, his wondrous creativity, and a myriad of remarkable contributions to the philosophy of democracy and the legacy of freethought, which he so richly endowed. Truly, Thomas Jefferson is one of the great benefactors of the race— the human race, and we would do well to revive his legacy whenever it focuses on our liberties, the importance of universal education, the advancement of science, and the primacy of reason in the conduct of human affairs, especially in the role of a responsible and responsive government in a free society.

An interesting coincidence, which comes under the heading of Jeffersonian trivia, is the fact that he and John Adams, lifelong political adversaries but friends who corresponded regularly, died hours apart on *July 4, 1826*—fifty years after the signing of the Declaration of Independence. It is said that Adams's last words were, "Thomas Jefferson lives," whereas, in fact, Jefferson had died two hours earlier! Five years later, on July 4, 1831, another former president and hero of the Revolutionary War, James Monroe, died!

January

January 1

We hold these truths to be self evident, that all men are created equal and independent; that from that equal creation they derive inherent and inalienable rights, among which are life, liberty, and the pursuit of happiness.*

Phillips Russell, *Jefferson, Champion of the Free Mind*
(New York: Dodd, Mead and Co., 1956), p. 37

January 2

We prevailed so far only as to repeal the laws which rendered criminal the maintenance of any religious opinions, the forbearance of repairing to church, or the exercise of any mode of worship; and further to exempt dissenters from contributions to the support of the established church. (Dec. 1776).

Autobiography, vol. 1, p. 39

---

*Jefferson's *first* draft of the Declaration of Independence had no reference to "God." It was what sprung to his mind first, a spontaneous recitation.

January 3

In every session from 1776 to 1779 a bill was discussed requiring everyone by a general assessment to support the pastor of his choice. The question against a general assessment was finally carried and the establishment of the Anglican Church entirely put down.

Ibid., vol. 1, p. 39

January 4

Although a majority of our citizens were dissenters, as has been observed, a majority of the legislature were church-men. Among these, however, were some reasonable and liberal men, who enabled us, on some points to obtain feeble majorities. (1776)

Ibid., vol. 1, p. 39

January 5

The restoration of the rights of conscience relieved the people from taxation for the support of a religion not theirs.

Ibid., vol. 1, p. 49

January 6

The bill for establishing religious freedom, the principles of which had to a certain degree been enacted before, I had drawn in all the latitude of reason and right. It still met with opposition; but with some mutilations in the preamble it was finally passed. . . . An amendment was proposed, by inserting the words

"Jesus Christ", so that it should read, "a departure from the plan of Jesus Christ, the holy author of our religion." The insertion was rejected by a great majority in proof that they meant to comprehend, within the mantle of its protection, the Jew and the Gentile, the Christian and the Mahometan, the Hindoo and the infidel of every denomination.

Ibid., vol. l, p. 45

January 7

The truth of Voltaire's observation offers itself perpetually . . . every man in France must be either the hammer or the anvil. It is a true picture of that country to which they say we shall pass hereafter, and where we are to see God and his angels in splendor, the crowds of the damned trampled under their feet.

Letter to Mr. Bellini, Paris, 1785

January 8

Our civil rights have no dependence on our religious opinions.

Appendix to *Notes on the State of Virginia*—
an Act for Establishing Religious Freedom,
passed in the Assembly of Virginia in 1786, p. 455

January 9

To compel a man to furnish contributions of money for the propagation of opinions he disbelieves, is sinful and tyrannical.

Ibid., p. 454

January 10

To suffer the civil magistrate to intrude his powers into the field of opinion and to restrain the propagation of principles on the supposition of their ill tendency, is a dangerous fallacy, which at once destroys all religious liberty.

Ibid.

January 11

Truth is great and will prevail if left to herself, she is the proper and sufficient antagonist to error and has nothing to fear from the conflict, unless by human interposition disarmed of her natural weapons—free argument and debate.

Ibid.

January 12

Constraint may make a man worse by making him a hypocrite but it will never make him a truer man. It may fix him obstinately in his errors but it will not cure them. Reason and free inquiry are the only effectual agents against error.

Notes on the State of Virginia, vol. 8, p. 400

January 13

With respect to the State of Virginia in particular, the people seem to have laid aside the monarchical and taken up the republican government, with as much ease as would attend their throwing off the old and putting on a new suit of clothes.

Letter to Benjamin Franklin, 1777

January 14

The system of money-arithmetic proposed would be entirely unmanageable for the common purposes of society. I proposed therefore, instead of this, to adopt the Dollar as our Unit of account and payment and that its divisions and subdivisions should be in the decimal state.

Autobiography, vol. l, p. 53

January 15

Our body was little numerous but very contentious. Day after day was wasted on most unimportant questions. It is really more questionable, than many at first thought, whether Bonaparte's dumb legislature, which said nothing but did much, may not be preferable to one which talks much and does nothing.

Ibid., vol. l, p. 58

January 16

It is of great importance to set a resolution, not to be shaken, never to tell an untruth. There is no vice so mean, so pitiful, so contemptible and he who permits himself to tell a lie once finds it much easier to do a second and a third time, till at length it becomes a habitual.

Letter to nephew Peter Carr, 1785

January 17

Our act for freedom of religion is extremely applauded. The ambassadors of this court have asked me for copies of it to send to their sovereigns and it is inserted full-length in the new encyclopedia.

Letter (from Paris) to Mr. Wythe, 1786

January 18

By far the most important bill in our whole code is the diffusion of knowledge among the people. No other sure foundation can be devised for the preservation of freedom and happiness.

Ibid.

January 19

If anybody thinks that the kings, nobles, or priests are good conservators of the public happiness, send him to Paris. It is the best school in the universe to cure him of that folly.

Ibid.

January 20

It is comfortable to see the standard of reason at length erected, after so many ages during which the human mind has been held in vassalage by kings, priests and nobles. . . . It is honorable for us to have produced the first legislature who had the courage to declare that the reason of a man may be trusted with the formation of his own opinions.

Letter to James Madison, 1786

January 21

Experience declares that man is the only animal which devours his own kind, for I can apply no milder term to governments of Europe and to the general prey of the rich on the poor.

Letter to Colonel E. Carrington, 1787

January 22

I congratulate you on the law of your state [South Carolina] for suspending the importation of slaves and for the glory you have justly acquired by endeavoring to prevent it forever. This abomination must have an end.

Letter to E. Rutledge, Esq., 1787

January 23

Fix reason in her seat and call to her tribunal every fact, every opinion. Question with boldness even the existence of a God because if there be one he must approve more of the homage of reason than that of blindfolded fear.

Letter to nephew Peter Carr, 1787

January 24

The legitimate powers of government extend to such acts only as are injurious to others. . . . It does me no injury for my neighbor to say there are twenty gods or no God, it neither picks my pocket nor breaks my leg.

Notes on the State of Virginia, vol. 8, p. 400

January 25

If it were left to me to decide whether we should have a government without newspapers or newspapers without a government, I should not hesitate a moment to prefer the latter. But
I should mean that every man receive those papers and be
capable of reading them.

Letter to Colonel E. Carrington, 1787

January 26

But this momentous question [the Missouri Compromise],*
like a fireball in the night, awakened and filled me with terror.
I considered it at once as the knell of the Union. It is hushed
indeed for the moment, but this is a reprieve only, not a final
sentence. A geographical line, coinciding with a marked principle once conceived and held up by angry passions of men will
never be obliterated and every new irritation will make it
deeper and deeper.

Letter to John Holmes, 1820

January 27

I do not like the omission of a bill of rights providing clearly
and without the aid of sophism for freedom of religion and
freedom of the press. . . . A bill of rights is what the people are
entitled to against every government on earth, general or par-

---

*The Missouri Compromise was one of several attempts by Congress to
solve the slavery issue. It was succeeded by the Kansas/Nebraska Act (1854)
and ultimately, when all attempts to solve the slavery issue by compromise
had failed, by the Civil War. The "knell of the Union" that Jefferson felt was
to prove a well-placed fear.

ticular, and what no government should refuse or rest on inference.

Letter to James Madison, 1787,
concerning the new U.S. Constitution
about to be submitted to the states for ratification*

January 28

The second feature I strongly dislike is the abandonment . . . of the principle of rotation in office and most particularly in the case of the President. Reason and experience tell us that the first magistrate will always be re-elected if he may be re-elected. He then is an officer for life. . . . Educate and inform the whole mass of the people. . . . They are the only sure reliance for the preservation of our liberty.

Ibid., 1787

January 29

I am very sensible to the honor you propose to me of becoming a member of the society for the abolition of the slave trade. You know that nobody wishes more ardently to see an abolition, not only of the trade but of the condition of slavery. . . . Certainly no one will be more willing to encounter every sacrifice for that object.

Letter to M. Warville, 1788

---

*As Jefferson was serving as U.S. Minister to France, he did not attend the Constitutional Convention. Madison became a prime mover in the formulation, promotion, and adoption of the Bill of Rights.

January 30

I was much an enemy of monarchies before I came to Europe. I am ten thousand times more so since I have seen what they are. . . . There is not a crowned head in Europe whose talents or merits would entitle him to be elected a vestryman by the people of any parish in America.

Letter to General George Washington, 1788

January 31

It is always better to have no ideas than false ones; to believe nothing than to believe what is wrong.

Letter to James Madison, 1788

February

February 1

The example we have given the world is single, that of changing our form of government under the authority of reason only, without bloodshed.

Letter to Mr. Izard, 1788

February 2

I concur with you strictly in your opinion of the comparative merits of atheism and demonism, and really see nothing but the latter in the being worshipped by many who think themselves Christians.

Letter to Dr. Price, 1789

February 3

Difference of opinion is advantageous in religion. The different sects perform the function of a censor morum over each other.

Notes on the State of Virginia, vol. 8, p. 401

February 4

I never had an opinion in politics or religion which I was afraid to own. A costove reserve on these subjects might have procured me more esteem from some people but less from myself.

Letter to F. Hopkington, 1789

February 5

I never submitted the whole system of my opinions to the creed of any party of men whatever, in religion, in philosophy, in politics or in anything else, where I was capable of thinking for myself. Such an addiction is the last degradation of a free and moral agent.

Ibid.

February 6

There are rights which it is useless to surrender to the government and which governments have yet always been able to invade. These are the rights of thinking and publishing our thoughts by speaking or writing; the right of free commerce; the right of personal freedom.

Letter to Colonel Humphreys, 1789

February 7

I know of but one code of morality for men whether acting singly or collectively.

Letter to James Madison, 1789

February 8

It is error alone which needs the support of government, truth can stand by itself.

Notes on the State of Virginia, vol. 8, p. 401

February 9

We are not to expect to be translated from despotism to liberty in a feather-bed.

Letter to Marquis de Lafayette, 1790

February 10

It takes time to persuade men to do even what is for their own good.

Letter to Charles Clay, 1790

February 11

It had become an universal and almost uncontroverted position in the several states that the purposes of society do not require a surrender of all our rights to our ordinary governors.

. . . Of the first kind, for instance, is freedom of religion, of the second, trial by jury, habeas corpus laws, free presses.

Letter to Noah Webster, 1790

February 12

Reason and persuasion are the only practical instruments against error. To make way for these, free inquiry must be indulged.

Notes on the State of Virginia, vol. 8, p. 401

February 13

I would rather be exposed to the inconveniences attending too much liberty than those attending too small a degree of it.

Letter to Mr. Stuart, 1791

February 14

Responsibility is a tremendous engine in a free government.

Ibid.

February 15

I am for freedom of religion and against all maneuvers to bring about a legal ascendancy of one sect over another; for freedom of the press and against all violations of the Constitution to silence by force and not by reason the complaints or criticism, just or unjust, of our citizens against their agents.

Letter to Elbridge Gerry, 1799

February 16

When the clergy addressed Gen. Washington on his departure from the government, it was observed in the consultation that he had never on any occasion said a word to the public which showed a belief in the Christian religion and they thought they should so pen their address as to force him, at length, to declare publicly whether he was a Christian or not. They did so. However, Dr. Rush observed, the old fox was too cunning for them. He answered every article of their address particularly, except that—which he passed over without notice.

The Annals, vol. 9, p. 198

February 17

Gouverneur Morris, who pretended to be in his secrets and believed himself to be so, has often told me that Gen. Washington believed no more of that system (the Christian religion) than he did himself.

Ibid.

February 18

Is uniformity(in religion) obtainable? Millions of innocent men, women and children, since the introduction of Christianity, have been burnt, tortured, fined, imprisoned, yet we have not advanced one inch toward uniformity.

Notes on the State of Virginia, vol. 8, p. 401

February 19

Though the will of the majority is in all cases to prevail, that will to be rightful must be reasonable; the minority possess their equal rights which equal laws must protect and to violate which would be oppression.

First Inaugural Address, 1801

February 20

Some have made the love of God the foundation of morality. Whence, then, arises the morality of the Atheist? . . . Diderot, D'Alembert, D'Holbach, Condorcet, are known to have been among the most virtuous of men. Their virtue then, must have had some other foundation than the love of God.

Letter to Thomas Law, 1814

February 21

Self-interest, or rather self-love, or egoism, has been more plausibly substituted as the basis of morality. But I consider our relations with others as constituting the boundaries of morality.

Ibid.

February 22

I never will, by any word or act, bow to the shrine of intolerance, or admit a right of inquiry into the religious opinions of others.

Letter to E. Dowse, 1803

February 23

My theory has always been that if we are to dream, the flatteries of hope are as cheap and pleasanter than the gloom of despair.

> Letter to M. DeMarbois, 1817

February 24

I have the consolation of having added nothing to my private fortune during my public service . . . of retiring with hands as clean as they are empty.

> Letter to M. le Comte Diodati, 1807

February 25

We have solved by fair experiment the great and interesting question whether freedom of religion is compatible with order in government and obedience to law. . . . We have experienced the quiet as well as the comfort which results from leaving every one to profess freely and openly those principles of religion which are the inductions of his own reason and the serious convictions of his own inquiries.

> Response to six Baptist associations of Virginia, 1808

February 26

But a short time elapsed after the death of the great reformer of the Jewish religion before his principles were departed from by those who professed to be his special servants and perverted into an engine for enslaving mankind and aggrandizing their oppressors in Church and State.

> Letter to Samuel Kercheval, 1810

February 27

The poor Quakers were flying from persecution in England. They cast their eyes on these new countries as asylums of civil and religious liberty but they found them free only for the reigning sect.

> *Notes on the State of Virginia*, vol. 7, p. 398

February 28

I consider the government of the United States as interdicted by the Constitution from intermeddling with religious institutions, their doctrines, disciplines or exercises. . . . Civil powers alone have been given to the President of the United States and no authority to direct the religious exercises of his constituents.

> Letter to Reverend Miller in answer to a petition
> that the president should appoint
> a national Thanksgiving Day, 1808

March

March 1

Truth and reason are eternal. They have prevailed and they will eternally prevail, however, in times and places they may be overborne for a while by violence, military, civil or ecclesiastical.

Letter to Reverend Mr. Knox, 1810

March 2

I have never been able to conceive how any rational being could propose happiness to himself from the exercise of power over others.

Letter to M. D. Tracy, 1811

March 3

I may sometimes differ in opinion from some of my own friends, from those whose views are as pure and sound as my own. I censure none but do homage to every one's right of opinion.

Letter to Colonel William Duane, 1811

March 4

Our opinions are not voluntary. Every man's reason must be his own oracle.

Letter to Dr. Benjamin Rush, 1813

March 5

About facts, you and I cannot differ because truth is our mutual guide. And if any opinions you express should be different from mine I shall receive them with the liberality and indulgence which I may ask for my own.

Letter to John Adams, 1813

March 6

Sweep away their gossamer fabrics of factitious religion and they would catch no more flies. We should all then live like the Quakers, live without an order of priests, moralize for ourselves, follow the oracle of conscience, and say nothing about what no man can understand, nor therefore believe, for I suppose belief to be the assent of the mind to an intelligible proposition.

Letter to John Adams, 1813

March 7

Opinion, and the just maintenance of it, shall never be a crime in my view, nor bring injury on the individual.

Letter to Samuel Adams, 1801

March 8

In the New Testament there is internal evidence that parts of it have proceeded from an extraordinary mind and that other parts are the fabric of very inferior minds.

Letter to John Adams, 1814

March 9

The last hope of human liberty in this world rests on us. We ought, for so dear a state, to sacrifice every attachment and every enmity. If we move in mass . . . we shall obtain our object . . . if we break into squads, every one pursuing the path he thinks most direct, we become an easy conquest to those who can now barely hold us in check.

Letter to Colonel William Duane, 1811

March 10

I have resumed the study of mathematics with great avidity. It was ever my favorite one. We have no theories there, no uncertainties remain on the mind; all is demonstration and satisfaction.

Letter to Dr. Benjamin Rush, 1811

March 11

The uniform tenor of a man's life furnishes better evidence of what he has said or done . . . than the word of an enemy . . . who shows that he prefers the use of falsehoods which suit him to truths which do not.

Letter to Governor Clinton, 1803

March 12

I believe in the general existence of a moral instinct. I think it the brightest gem with which the human character is studded and the want of it as more degrading than the most hideous of the bodily deformities.

Letter to Thomas Law, 1814

March 13

Of publishing a book on religion I never had an idea. I should as soon think of writing for the reformation of Bedlam as of the world of religious sects. Of these, there must be at least ten thousand, every individual of every one of which believes all wrong but his own.

Letter to Charles Class, 1815

March 14

We have borne patiently a great deal of wrong [for] . . . if nations go to war for every degree of injury there would never be peace on earth. . . . When wrongs are pressed because it is believed they will be borne, resistance becomes morality.

Letter to Madame de Stael de Holstein, 1807

March 15

I hope our wisdom will grow with our power and teach us that the less we use our power the greater it will be.

Letter to Mr. Leiper, 1815

March 16

Believing that a representative government responsible at short periods of election is that which produces the greatest sum of happiness to mankind . . . I should unwillingly be the person, who disregarding the sound precedent set by an illustrious predecessor, should furnish the first example of prolongation beyond the second term of office.

To the General Assembly of North Carolina, 1808

March 17

They [the Christian Platonists] have compounded from the heathen mysteries a system beyond the comprehension of man, of which the great reformer of the vicious ethics and deism of the Jews, were he to return on earth, would not recognize one feature.

Letter to Charles Thompson, 1816

March 18

I have ever judged of the religion of others by their lives. By the same test the world must judge me.

Letter to Mrs. M. Harrison Smith, 1816

March 19

Laws and institutions must go hand in hand with the progress of the human mind. As that becomes more developed, more enlightened, as new discoveries are made, new truths disclosed . . . institutions must advance also and keep pace with the times.

Letter to Samuel Kercheval, 1816

March 20

[I]n the age of Aristotle they had just ideas of the value of personal liberty but none at all of the structure of government best calculated to preserve it. . . . The full experiment of a government democratical but representative was and is still reserved for us.

Letter to Mr. Issac H. Tiffany, 1816

March 21

I believe that the moral sense is as much a part of our constitution as that of feeling, seeing or hearing.

Letter to John Adams, 1816

March 22

The result of your forty or sixty years of religious reading, in the four words, "Be just and good" is that which all our inquiries must end.

Letter to John Adams, 1817

March 23

Say nothing of my religion. It is known to my god and myself alone. Its evidence before the world is to be sought in my life. If that has been honest and dutiful to society, the religion that has regulated it cannot be a bad one.

Ibid.

March 24

If by religion we are to understand sectarian dogmas, in which no two of them agree, then your exclamation on the hypothesis is just, "that this would be the best of all possible worlds if there were no religion in it."

Letter to John Adams, 1817

March 25

All men should be free to profess by argument to maintain their opinions in matters of religion and the same in no way should diminish, enlarge, or effect their civil capacities.

Appendix to *Notes on the State of Virginia*, vol. 8, p. 455

March 26

After all, men of character must have enemies because there are two sides to every question and taking one with decision and acting on it with effect, those who take the other will of course be hostile in proportion as they feel the effect.

Letter to John Adams, 1817

March 27

You say you are a Calvinist. I am not. I am a sect by myself as far as I know. I am not a Jew and therefore do not adopt their theology which supposes the god of infinite justice to punish the sins of the fathers upon their children unto the third and fourth generation.

Letter to Ezra Stiles, 1819

March 28

The immaculate conception of Jesus, his deification . . . his miraculous powers, his resurrection and visible ascension, his corporeal presence in the Eucharist, the Trinity, original sin, atonement, regeneration, election orders of Hierarchy etc. have resulted from artificial systems.

Letter to William Short, 1819

March 29

I am tired of practical politics and am happier while reading the history of ancient than of modern times. The total banishment of all moral principle from the code which governs the intercourse of nations . . . sickens my soul unto death.

Letter to Colonel William Duane, 1813

March 30

You may have heard the hue and cry raised from the different pulpits on our appointment of Dr. Cooper [to the College of William and Mary], whom they charge with Unitarianism as boldly as if they knew the fact and as presumptuously as if it were a crime and one for which, like Servetus, he should be burned.

Letter to General Taylor, 1820

March 31

If we could believe that Jesus really countenanced the follies, the falsehoods, and the charlatans which his biographers father on him and admit the misconstructions, interpolations and theorizations of the fathers of the early and the fanatics of the latter ages, the conclusion would be irresistible by every sound mind, that he was an imposter.

Letter to William Short, 1829

April

April 1

The clergy and nobility, as clergy and nobility eternally will, are opposed to giving to the Tiers Etat* so effectual a representation as may dismount them from their backs.

Letter to Mr. Carmichael, December 25, 1788

April 2

I never go to bed without an hour or half hour's previous reading of something moral, whereon to ruminate in the intervals of sleep. But whether I retire to bed early or late, I rise with the sun.

Letter to Dr. Vine Utley, who had written Jefferson asking for information on his physical habits, 1819

---

*Is it not interesting that on Christmas Day, Jefferson would have such a disparaging comment on the clergy?

April 3

Self-love, therefore, is no part of morality. Indeed it is exactly its counterpart. It is the sole antagonist of virtue, leading us to constantly by our propensities to self-gratification in violation of our moral duties to others.

Letter to Thomas Law, 1814

April 4

When I meet a proposition beyond finite comprehension, I abandon it as I do a weight which human strength cannot lift. . . . I think ignorance, in these cases, to be the softest pillow on which I can lay my head.

Letter to John Adams, 1820

April 5

[O]f this band of dupes and impostors, Paul was the great Coryphaeus* and first corrupter of Jesus.

Letter to William Short, 1820

April 6

This syllabus is meant to place the character of Jesus in its true and high light, as no imposter himself but a great reformer of the Hebrew code of religion. . . . It is not to be understood that I am with him in all of his doctrines. I am a Materialist; he takes the side of Spiritualism.

Letter to William Short, 1820

*Leader of the chorus in ancient Greek drama.

April 7

How many of our wisest men still believe in the reality of inspirations while perfectly sane on all other subjects.

Ibid.

April 8

Where there is an absence of matter I call it *void* or *nothing* or *immaterial space*. . . . To talk of *immaterial existences* is to talk of *nothings*.

Letter to John Adams, 1820

April 9

As members of the universal society of mankind and standing in high and responsible relation with them, it is our sacred duty to suppress passion among ourselves and not to blast the confidence we have, inspired of proof, that a government of reason is better than one of force.

Letter to Richard Rush, 1820

April 10

The metaphysical insanities of Ignatius of Loyola and of Calvin, are to my understanding mere lapses into polytheism differing from paganism only by being more unintelligible.

Letter to Rev. Jared Sparks, 1820

April 11

If the freedom of religion, guaranteed to us by law in *theory* can ever rise *in practise* under the overbearing inquisition of public opinion, truth will prevail.

Ibid.

April 12

Let us hope that the human mind will some day get back to the freedom it enjoyed two thousand years ago. . . . The inquisition of public opinion overwhelms in practise the freedom asserted by the laws in theory.

Letter to John Adams, 1821

April 13

When we shall have done away the incomprehensible jargon of the Trinitarian arithmetic, that three are one and one is three, when we shall have knocked down the artificial scaffolding reared to mask from view the simple structure of Jesus; when—in short—we shall have unlearned everything that has been taught since his day and got back to the pure and simple doctrines he inculcated, we shall then be truly and worthily his disciples.

Letter to Timothy Pickering, 1821

April 14

The blasphemy and absurdity of the five points of Calvin and the impossibility of defending them render their advocates impatient of reasoning, irritable, and prone to denunciation.

Letter to Dr. Cooper, 1822

April 15

In our university there is no Professor of Divinity. A handle has been made of this to disseminate an idea that this is an institution not merely of no religion but against all religions. . . . We suggested the expediency of encouraging the different religious sects to establish, each for itself, a professorship of their own tenets on the confines of the university. . . , preserving their independence of us and of each other.

Ibid.

April 16

The hocus-pocus phantasm of a God like another Cerberus, with one body and three heads, had its birth and growth in the blood of thousands and thousands of martyrs.

Letter to James Smith, 1822

April 17

Man once surrendering his reason has no remaining guard against absurdities. . . . Gullibility, which they call faith, takes the helm from the hand of reason and the mind becomes a wreck.

Ibid.

April 18

I can never join Calvin in addressing *his* God. . . . If ever a man worshipped a God he did . . . it would be more pardonable to believe in no God at all than to blaspheme him by the attributes of Calvin.

Letter to John Adams, 1823

April 19

The day will come when the mystical generation of Jesus by the Supreme Being as his father in the womb of a virgin, will be classed with the fable of Minerva in the brain of Jupiter.

Ibid.

April 20

I do not know that it is a duty to disturb by missionaries the religion and peace of other countries who may think of themselves bound to extinguish by fire and faggot heresies to which we give the name of conversions and quote our own example for it.

Letter to Mr. Megear, 1823

April 21

Our institution [William and Mary] will allow students uncontrolled choice in the lectures they shall choose to attend. It will proceed on the principle of doing all the good it can without consulting its own pride or ambition . . . letting everyone come and listen to whatever he thinks may improve the condition of his mind.

Letter to George Ticknor , 1823

April 22

Laws are made for men of ordinary understanding and should, therefore, be constructed by the ordinary rules of common sense. Their meaning is not to be sought for in metaphysical subtleties, which may make anything mean everything or nothing—at pleasure.

Letter to Judge Johnson, 1823

April 23

Eternal Vigilance is the Price of Liberty.*

Inscribed on the National Archives Building
in Washington, D.C.

April 24

I do not consider it as revelations of the Supreme Being, whom I would not so far blaspheme as to impute to him a pretension

---

*While this quotation is often attributed to Jefferson it does not appear in any of Jefferson's writings. The quotation bearing the most resemblance to the one above comes from an Irish politician, J. P. Curran, who in 1790 declared: "The condition upon which God hath given liberty to man is eternal vigilance." There is no reason to doubt that Jefferson would have endorsed Curran's observation, for the sentiment is surely reflected in dozens of Jefferson's utterances!

of revelation, couched in . . . terms which he would know, were never to be understood by those to whom they were addressed.

Letter to General Alexander Smith, 1825

April 25

The general spread of the light of science has already opened to every view the palpable truth that the mass of man has not been born with saddles on their backs, nor a favored few booted and spurred, ready to ride them legitimately by the grace of God.

Letter to Mr. Weightman, 1826

April 26

Our sister states of Pennsylvania and New York have long subsisted without any [church] establishment . . . the experiment was new and doubtful when they made it. It has answered beyond conception. . . . They have made the happy discovery that the way to silence religious disputes is to take no notice of them.

Notes on the State of Virginia, vol. 3, p. 265

April 27

The clergy by getting themselves established by law and ingrafted into the machine of government have been a very formidable engine against the civil and religious rights of man. They are still so in many countries and even in some of these United States. Even in 1783, we doubted the stability of our recent measures for reducing them to the footings of other useful callings.

Letter to Jeremiah Moore, 1800

April 28

Declining higher objects, my only one must be to show that suggestion and fact are different things . . . that public misfortune may be produced as well by public poverty and private disobedience to laws, as by the misconduct of public servants.

Letter to the Marquis de Lafayette, 1781

April 29

I think that by far the most important bill in our whole code is that for diffusion of knowledge among the people. No other sure foundation can be devised for the preservation of freedom and happiness. . . . Preach, my dear sir, a crusade against ignorance; establish and improve the law for educating the common people . . . The tax that will be paid for this purpose is not more than the thousandth part of what will be paid to kings, priests, and nobles who will rise up among us if we leave the people in ignorance.

Letter to George Wythe, 1786

April 30

Your letter found me a little emerging from the stupor of mind which rendered me as dead to the world as was she whose loss occasioned it. . . . If you should have thought me remiss you will, I am sure, ascribe it to its true cause, the state of dreadful suspense in which I have been kept all summer and the catastrophe which causes it.*

Letter to the Chevalier de Chattellux, 1782

*The death of Mrs. Jefferson

May

May 1

For it is in our lives and not from our words that our religion must be read. By the same test the world must judge me. But this does not satisfy the priesthood. They must have a positive, declared assent to all their interest in absurdities. My opinion is that there never would have been an infidel if there never had been a priest. The artificial structures they have built on the purest of all moral systems for the purpose of deriving from it pence and power, revolts those who think for themselves and who read in the system only what really is there.

Letter to Mrs. Harrison Smith, 1813

May 2

I am really mortified to be told that, in the United States of America, a fact like this can become a subject of inquiry and a criminal inquiry too as an offense against religion, that a question about the sale of a book can be carried before the civil magistrate. Is this then our freedom of religion? Are we to have a censor whose imprimatur shall say what books may be sold and what we may buy? And who is thus to dogmatize religious opinions for our citizens? Whose foot is to be the measure to which ours are to be cut or stretched . . . ? If M. de Becourt's book be false in its facts, disprove them; if false in its reasoning, refute it. But for God's sake, let us freely hear both sides. . . .

Letter to M. Dufief, 1814

May 3

The care of every man's soul belongs to himself. But what if he neglect the care of his health or estate, which more nearly relate to the state? Will the magistrate make a law that he shall not be poor or sick? Laws provide against injury from others, but not from ourselves. . . . God himself will not save men against their wills.

Notes on Religion, 1776, vol. 2, p. 100

May 4

After the year 1800 . . . there shall be neither slavery nor involuntary servitude in any of the said states.*

Notes on Religion, vol. 3, p. 432

---

*From a proposal submitted to the Continental Congress (1784) outlining a plan of government for western territory. Had Jefferson's proposal been adopted, slavery would have been excluded from *all* the admitted states of the Confederation. Regrettably, his proposal failed by *one vote!*

May 5

I considered, and now consider, that law [Alien and Sedition law] to be a nullity, as absolute and palpable as if Congress had ordered us to fall down and worship a golden image. . . . It was as much my duty to arrest its execution in every stage as it would have been to have rescued from the fiery furnace those who have been cast in to it for refusing to worship their image.

Letter to Mrs. John Adams, 1787

May 6

No government ought to be without censors and when the press is free, no one ever will. Nature has given to man no other means of sifting out the truth either in religion, law or politics. I think it is as honorable to the government neither to know nor notice its sycophants or censors as it would be undignified and criminal to pamper the former and persecute the latter.

Letter to President George Washington, 1792

May 7

The spirit of resistance to government is so valuable on certain occasions that I wish it always to be kept alive. It will often be exercised when wrong but better so than not to be exercised at all. I like a little rebellion now and then. It is like a storm in the atmosphere.

Letter to Mrs. John Adams, 1787

May 8

If there be those among us who would destroy this union or change its republican form, let them stand undisturbed as monuments to the safety of which error of opinion may be tolerated where reason is left free to combat it.

First Inaugural Address, 1801

May 9

No freeman shall be deprived the use of arms within his own lands. There shall be no standing army but in time of war.

From a proposed constitution for Virginia, 1776

May 10

What country before ever existed a century and a half without a rebellion? And what country can preserve its liberties, if its rulers are not warned from time to time that this people preserve the spirit of resistance? Let them take arms. The remedy is to set them right as to facts, pardon and pacify them. What signify a few lives lost in a century or two? The tree of liberty must be refreshed from time to time with the blood of tyrants. It is its natural manure.

Letter to Colonel Smith, 1787

May 11

I sincerely rejoice at the acceptance of our new constitution by nine states. It is a good canvass on which some strokes only want retouching. What these are . . . calls for a bill of rights. It seems pretty generally understood that this should go to juries, habeas corpus, standing armies, printing, religion and monopolies. . . . It is better to establish trials by jury, the right of habeas corpus, freedom of the press and freedom of religion— in all cases—than not to do it in any. . . . I hope therefore a bill of rights will be formed to guard the people against the federal government as they are already guarded against their state governments in most instances.

Letter to James Madison, 1788

May 12

Gentlemen*. . . . Your residence in the United States has given you an opportunity of becoming acquainted with the extremes of freedom of the press in these states. Considering its great importance to the public liberty and the difficulty of subjecting to very precise rules, the laws have thought it less mischievous to give greater scope to its freedom than to the restraint of it.

Letter to Messers. DeVair and Jaudens, 1793

May 13

I do not believe it is for the interest of religion to invite the civil magistrate to direct its exercises, its disciplines or its doctrines, nor of religious societies that the general government should be invested with the power of effecting any uniformity of time or matter among them. Fasting and prayer are religious exercises; the enjoining them an act of discipline. Every religious society has a right to determine for itself the times of

*Official representatives from Spain.

these exercises and the objects proper for them according to their particular tenets. . . . This right can never be safer than in their own hands, where the constitution has deposited it.

Letter to Samuel Miller, 1808

May 14

I have often thought that nothing would do more extensive good at small expense than the establishment of a small circulating library in every county. . . . I always hear with pleasure of institutions for promotion of knowledge among my countrymen. . . . Should your example lead to this, it will do great good.

Letter to John Wyche, 1809

May 15

Equal and exact justice to all men . . . freedom of religion, freedom of the press, freedom of person under the protection of habeas corpus . . . trial by juries impartially selected—these principles form the bright constellation which has gone before us.

First Inaugural Address, 1801

May 16

Yet I will not believe our labors are lost. I shall not die without a hope that light and liberty are on steady advance. . . . Flames kindled on the 4th of July, 1776, have spread over too much of the globe to be extinguished by the feeble engines of despotism. On the contrary, they will consume these engines and all those who work them.

Letter to John Adams, 1821

May 17

I rejoice as a moralist at the prospect of the reduction of the duties on wine by our national legislature. . . . No nation is drunken where wine is cheap and none sober where the dearness of wine substitutes ardent spirits as the common beverage. It is, in truth, the only antidote to the bane of whiskey.

Letter to M. DeNeuville, 1818

May 18

In every government on earth there is some trace of human weakness, some germ of corruption and degeneracy, which cunning will discover and wickedness insensibly open, cultivate and improve.

Notes on the State of Virginia, vol. 8, p. 390

May 19

The Jews presented for the object of their worship, a being of terrific character, cruel, vindictive, capricious and unjust.

Letter to William Short, 1820

May 20

That Jesus did not mean to impose himself on mankind as the son of God, physically speaking, I have been convinced by the writings of men more learned than myself in that lore. But that he might conscientiously believed himself inspired from above is very possible.

Ibid.

May 21

You ask my opinion of Lord Bolingbrooke and Thomas Paine. They were alike in making bitter enemies of priests and pharisees of their day. Both were honest men, both advocates for human liberty.

Letter to Francis Eppes, 1821

May 22

Let us hope the human mind will some day get back to the freedom it enjoyed two thousand years ago. This country, which has given the world the example of physical liberty, owes to it that of moral emancipation also, for as yet it is but nominal with us. The inquisition of public opinion overwhelms in practise the freedom asserted by laws in theory.

Letter to John Adams, 1821

May 23

I can say with truth that I never suffered a political to become a personal difference. I have been left on this ground by some friends whom I dearly loved but I was never the first to separate.

Letter to Timothy Pickering, 1821

May 24

The religion-builders have so distorted and deformed the doctrines of Jesus, so muffled them in mysticism, fancies and falsehoods, have caricatured them into forms so monstrous and inconceivable, as to shock reasonable thinkers to revolt against the whole and drive them rashly to pronounce the founder an imposter.

Ibid.

May 25

When all government, domestic and foreign, in little as well as great things, shall be drawn to Washington as the center of all power, it will render powerless the checks provided of one government on another and will become as venal and oppressive as the government from which we separated.

Letter to Mr. C. Hammond, 1821

May 26

When the friends of our youth are gone and a generation is risen around us and whom we know not—is death an evil?

Letter to John Adams, 1822

May 27

Unitarianism has not yet been preached to us [in Virginia] but the breeze begins to be felt which precedes the storm. Fanaticism is all in a bustle, shutting its doors and windows to keep it out. But it will come and drive before it the foggy mists of Platonism which have so long obscured our atmosphere.

Letter to Dr. Waterhouse, 1822

May 28

I think it should be a penitentiary felony to publish one's letters without leave. Yet, you will see that they draw me out into the arena of newspapers. Although I know it is too late for me to buckle on the armor of youth, yet, my indignation would not permit me passively to receive the kick of an ass.

Letter to John Adams, 1822

May 29

Our first and fundamental maxim should be: never entangle ourselves in the broils of Europe. Our second: never to suffer Europe to intermeddle with cis-Atlantic affairs.

Letter to President James Monroe, 1823*

May 30

Whether in writing the Declaration of Independence I had gathered my ideas from reading or reflection, I do not know. I know only that I turned to neither book nor pamphlet when writing it. I did not consider it part of my charge to invent new ideas altogether and to offer no sentiment which had ever been expressed before.

Letter to James Madison, 1823

---

*President Monroe's famous Monroe Doctrine reflected Jefferson's recommendation to his good friend, President Monroe.

May 31

Sometimes it is said that man cannot be trusted with the government of himself. Can he then be trusted with the government of others? Or have we found angels in the form of kings to govern him? Let history answer this question.

First Inaugural Address, 1801

June

June 1

Is there any such thing as happiness in this world ? No. And as for admiration, I am sure the man who powders most, perfumes most, embroiders most, and talks most nonsense, is most admired.

Letter to John Page,* 1762

June 2

This very day [December 25], to others the day of greatest mirth and jollity, seems to me overwhelmed with more and greater misfortunes than have befallen a descendant of Adam for these thousand years past, I am sure; and perhaps, after excepting Job, since the creation of the world.

Ibid.

---

*Jefferson's student at William and Mary.

June 3

I can scarcely contemplate a more incalculable evil than the breaking of the union into two or more parts.

Letter to President George Washington, 1792

June 4

The most fortunate of us, in our journey through life, frequently meet with calamities and misfortunes which may greatly afflict us; and to fortify our minds against them should be one of the principal studies and endeavors of our lives.

Letter to John Page, 1763

June 5

In 1769, I became a member of the legislature [of Virginia] . . . and made one effort in that body for the permission of emancipation of the slaves, which was rejected; and indeed, during the regal government, nothing liberal could expect success.

Autobiography, vol. 1, p. 3

June 6

Our minds were within narrow limits by an habitual belief that it was our duty to direct all our labors in subservience to her [England] interests and even to observe a bigoted intolerance for all religions but hers.

Ibid.

June 7

The great principles of right and wrong are legible to every reader. To pursue them requires not the aid of many counselors. [1774]

Ibid.

June 8

The whole of government consists in the art of being honest. . . . Only aim to do your duty and mankind will give you credit when you fail. [1774]

Ibid.

June 9

I sent a copy of my draught—The political relation between us and England [in 1775]—to Patrick Henry. Whether he disapproved the ground taken or was too lazy to read it (for he was the laziest man in reading I ever knew) I never learned. . . . He communicated it to no one.

Ibid., p. 8

June 10

Kings are the servants not the proprietors of the people. [1774]

Appendix to *Autobiography*, vol. 1, p. 141

June 11

Every citizen should be a soldier. This was the case with the Greeks and the Romans and must be that of every free state. When there is no oppression there will be no hirelings. We must train and classify the whole of our male citizens and make military instruction a regular part of collegiate education. We can never be safe until this is done.

Letter to Colonel James Monroe, 1813

June 12

We lay it down as a fundamental that laws to be just must give a reciprocation of right. . . . Without this they are mere arbitrary rules of conduct founded in force and not in conscience.

Notes on the State of Virginia, Query XIV, vol. 8, p. 385

June 13

If the present Congress [1782] errs in too much talking, how can it be otherwise in a body to which the people send one hundred and fifty lawyers, whose trade is to question everything.

Autobiography, vol. 1 p. 58

June 14

I served with General Washington in the legislature of Virginia before the revolution and during it with Dr. Franklin in Congress. I never heard either of them speak ten minutes at a time nor to any but the main point which was to decide the question. They laid their shoulders to the points knowing that the little ones would follow of themselves.

Autobiography, vol. 1, p. 58

June 15

Experience has shown that the hereditary branches of modern government are the patrons of privilege and prerogative and not of the natural rights of the people whose oppressors they generally are.

Letter to General George Washington, 1784

June 16

In the pleasure of the table the French are far before us because with good taste they unite temperance. . . . I have never seen a man drunk in France, even among the lowest of the people.

Letter to Mr. Bellini, 1785

June 17

You have formed a just opinion of Monroe. He is a man whose soul might be turned wrong side outward without discovering a blemish to the world.

Letter to W. T. Franklin, 1784

June 18

On the subject of an election by a general ticket, or by districts, most persons seem to have made up their minds. All agree that an election by districts would be best, if it could be general. . . . While ten states choose either by their legislatures or by a general ticket, it is folly and worse than folly for the other six not to do it.

Letter to James Monroe, 1800

June 19

To justify a conclusion requires many observations even where the subject may be submitted to the anatomical knife, to optical glasses, to analysis by fire and solvents. How much more then where it is a faculty, not a substance we are examining.

Notes on the State of Virginia, vol. 8, p. 386

June 20

I wish to heaven you may continue in the disposition to fix your house in Abermarle and perhaps Madison will be tempted to do so. This will be society enough and it will be the great sweetener of our lives. Without society and a society to our taste, men are never contented.

Letter to Colonel Monroe, 1786

June 21

I am convinced that those societies (as the Indians) which live without government, enjoy in their general mass an infinitely greater degree of happiness than those who live under European governments. Among the former, public opinion is in the place of law and restrains morals as powerfully as laws ever did anywhere.

Letter to Colonel Edward Carrington, 1787

June 22

Wretched, indeed, is the nation in whose affairs foreign powers are once permitted to intermeddle.

Letter to Mr. B. Vaughn, 1787

June 23

It is a source of infinite comfort to reflect that under every chance of fortune we have a resource in ourselves from which we are able to derive an honorable subsistence.

Letter to T. M. Randolph, Jr., 1787

June 24

I know of no remedy against indolence and extravagance but a free course of justice; everything else is merely palliative.

Letter to A. Donald, 1787

June 25

I rely on the good sense of the people for remedy whereas the evils of monarchical government are beyond remedy.

Letter to Dr. Ramsey, 1787

June 26

With all the imperfections of our present government it is without comparison the best existing—or that ever did exist.

Ibid.

June 27

It has been thought that corruption is restrained by confining of suffrage to a few of the wealthier people. . . . it would be more effectively restrained by an extension of that right to such numbers as would bid defiance to the means of corruption.

Notes on the State of Virginia, vol. 8, p. 391

June 28

With all the defects of our Constitution, whether general or particular, the comparison of our governments with those of Europe is like a comparison of heaven and hell.

Letter to Joseph Jones, 1787

June 29

My idea is that we should be made one nation in every case concerning foreign affairs and separate ones in whatever is domestic.

Letter to J. Blair, 1787

June 30

No race of kings has ever presented above one man of common sense in twenty generations.

Letter to Benjamin Hawkings, 1787

July

July 1

Cultivators of the earth are the most valuable citizens. They are the most vigorous, the most independent, the most virtuous, and they are tied to their country and wedded to its liberty and interest by lasting bonds.

Letter to John Jay, 1785

July 2

I consider the Alien and Sedition laws as merely an experiment of the American mind to see how far it will bear an avowed violation of the Constitution. If this goes down we shall immediately see attempted another act of Congress declaring the President shall continue in office during life reserving to another occasion the transfer of succession to his heirs and the establishment of the Senate for life.

Letter to S. T. Mason, 1798

July 3

Commerce with all nations, alliances with none should be our motto.

Letter to Thomas Lomax, 1799

July 4

Independence and the establishment of a new form of government, were not even in 1776 the objects of the people at large. The idea had not been opened to the mass of people in April; much less can it be said that they had made up their minds in its favor.

Notes on the State of Virginia, 1782

July 5

The real friends of the constitution in its federal form, if they wish it to be immortal, should be attentive by amendments to make it keep pace with the advance of the age in science and experience.

Letter to R. G. Garrett, 1824

July 6

I agree with you there is a natural aristocracy among men. The grounds of this are virtue and talents. . . . There is also an artificial aristocracy founded on wealth and birth without either virtue or talents.

Letter to John Adams, 1813

July 7

The Palladium is understood to be the clerical paper and from the clergy I expect no mercy. . . . The laws of the present day withhold their hands from blood but lies and slander still remain to them.

Letter to Levi Lincoln, 1801

July 8

Our interest will be to throw open the doors of commerce and to knock off its shackles, giving perfect freedom to all persons for the vent of whatever they may choose to bring into our ports and asking the same in theirs.

Notes on the State of Virginia, 1782

July 9

A government held together by the bands of reason only requires much compromise of opinion. . . . Things even salutary should not be crammed down the throats of dissenting brethren, especially when they may be put into a form to be willingly swallowed. . . . A great deal of indulgence is necessary to strengthen habits of harmony and fraternity.

Letter to Edward Livingston, 1824

July 10

Resolved unanimously that this Assembly of Virginia not listen to any proposition or suffer any negotiation inconsistent with their national faith and Federal union, and that a proposition from the enemy treating with any Assembly or body of men in America other than the Congress of these United States is insidious and inadmissable.

Resolution proposed by Jefferson
regarding peace with England in 1778*

July 11

Some men look at constitutions with sanctimonious reverence and deem them to be like the ark of the covenant, too sacred to be touched. They ascribe to men of a preceding age a wisdom more than human and suppose what they did to be beyond amendment. . . . I know . . . that laws and institutions must go hand in hand with the progress of the human mind. . . . We might as well require a man to wear still the coat that fitted him when a boy as civilized society to remain ever under the regimen of their barbarous ancestors. . . . Each generation is as independent of the one preceding as that was of all of which had gone before. . . . The dead have no rights. They are nothing and nothing cannot be something.

Letter to Samuel Kercheval, 1816

July 12

The way to make friends quarrel is to put them in disputation under the public eye. An experience of near twenty years has taught me that few friendships stand this test, and that public assemblies, where everyone is free to act and speak, are the most powerful looseners of the bands of private friendship.

Letter to George Washington, 1784

---

*This was *nine* years before the Constitution was written.

July 13

We have long suffered under base prostitutions of law to party passion in one judge, and the imbecility of another.

Letter to Governor Tyler, 1810

July 14

The clergy by getting themselves established by law and ingrafted into the machinery of government have been a very formidable engine against the civil and religious rights of man.

Letter to Jeremiah Moore, 1800

July 15

And as every sect believes its own form the true one, every one hopes for his home. . . . The returning good sense of our country threatens abortion to their hopes and they believe that any portion of power confided to me will be exerted in opposition to their schemes. And they believe rightly for I have sworn upon the altar of God eternal hostility against every form of tyranny over the mind of man. But this is all they have to fear from me . . . and this is the cause of their printing lying pamphlets against me.

Letter to Benjamin Rush, 1800

July 16

The ground of liberty is to be gained by inches; we must be contented to secure what we can get from time to time and eternally press forward for what is yet to get. It takes time to persuade men to do even what is for their own good.

Letter to the Reverend Charles Clay, 1790

July 17

Be it enacted by the General Assembly that on the first day of January, in every year, there shall be paid out of the treasury the sum of two thousand pounds to be laid out in such books and maps as are proper to be preserved in a public library and in defraying the expenses necessary for the care and preservation thereof.

From the Bill for Establishing a Public Library
in Richmond, Virginia, 1777

July 18

Experience has taught me that manufacturers are now as necessary to our independence as to our comfort. . . . If those who quote me as of a different opinion will keep pace with me in purchasing nothing foreign where an equivalent in domestic fabric can be obtained, without regard to a difference in price, it will not be our fault if we do not soon have a supply at home equal to our demand and wrest that weapon of distress from the hand that has wielded it.

Letter to Benjamin Austin, 1816

July 19

In every age the priest has been hostile to liberty. He is always in alliance with the despot, abetting his abuses in return for protection of his own. . . . They have perverted the best religion ever preached to man into mystery and jargon, unintelligible to all mankind and therefore the safer engine for their purposes.

Letter to H. G. Spafford, 1814

July 20

Our people, very good friend, are firm and unanimous in their principles of Republicanism and there is no better proof of it than that they love what you write and read it with delight.

Letter to Thomas Paine, 1779

July 21

Resolved that the money of these states . . . shall be divided into fractions decimally expressed. That there shall be coin of silver of the value of an unit, one other of the same metal of one-tenth of an unit, one other of copper of the value of the hundredth of an unit.

From a draft report presented to Congress, 1784

July 22

I agree with you entirely in condemning the mania of giving names to objects of any kind after persons still living. Death

alone can seal the title of any man to this honor by putting it
out of his power to forfeit it.

Letter to Benjamin Rush, 1800

July 23

Nobody wishes more than I do to see such proofs as you exhibit
that nature has given to our black brethren talents equal to
those of the other colors of men and that the appearance of
want of them is owing merely to the degraded condition of
their existence both in Africa and America. I can add with
truth that nobody wishes more ardently to see a good system
commenced for raising the condition of their body and mind to
what it ought to be.

Letter to Benjamin Bainecker, 1791

July 24

Were I to undertake to answer the calumnies of the newspapers
it would be more than all my time and twenty aides could effect.
For while I should be answering one, twenty new ones would be
invented. I have thought it better to trust the judgement of my
countrymen that they would judge me by what they see of my
conduct on the stage where they have placed me.

Letter to Samuel Smith, 1798

July 25

[E]ven if we differ in principle more than I believe we do, you
and I know too well the texture of the human mind and the
slipperiness of human reason to consider differences of opinion

otherwise than differences of form or feature. Integrity of views more than their soundness is the basis of esteem.

Letter to Elbridge Gerry, 1799

July 26

I have made it a rule to grant no pardon in any criminal case but on the recommendation of the judges who sat on the trial and the district attorney, or two of them. I believe it a sound rule and not to be departed from but in extraordinary cases.

Letter to Albert Gallitan, 1806

July 27

You say I must go to writing history. While in public life I had not time, and now that I am retired, I am past the time. To write history requires a whole life of observation, of inquiry, of labor and correction.

Letter to Dr. J. B. Stuart, 1817

July 28

It is not for me to pronounce on the hypothesis you present on the transmigration of souls from one body to another. . . . The laws of nature have withheld from us the means of physical knowledge of the country of spirits. . . . Revelation has, for reasons unknown to us, chosen to leave us in the dark.

Letter to Reverend Issac Story, 1801

July 29

Certainly an inventor ought to be allowed a right to the benefit of his invention for some certain time. It is equally certain it ought not to be perpetual. . . . To embarrass society with monopolies for every utensil existing . . . would be more injurious to them had the supposed inventors never existed.

Letter to Oliver Evans, 1807

July 30

It should be our endeavor to cultivate the peace and friendship of every nation, even of that which has injured us most, when we shall have carried our point against her. . . . Never has so much false arithmetic [been] employed on any subject as that which has been employed to persuade nations it is in their interest to go to war.

Notes on the State of Virginia, 1782

July 31

My opinion was that the President of the United States should be elected for seven years and forever ineligible afterwards. I have since become sensible that seven years is too long to be irremovable and that there should be a peaceable way of withdrawing a man in midway who is doing wrong. The service for eight years with the power to remove at the end of four, comes nearly to my principle as corrected by experience. . . . It is in adherence to that that I am determined to withdraw at the end of my second term. The danger is that the indulgence and attachment of the people will keep a man in the chair after he becomes a dotard.

Letter to John Taylor, 1805

August

August 1

How far does the duty of toleration extend? First, no church is bound by the duty of toleration to retain within her bosom obstinate offenders against her laws. Second, we have no right to prejudice another in civil employment because he is of another church. If any man err from the right way it is his own misfortune [and] no injury to thee. Nor art [thou] therefore to punish him in the things of this life because thou supposeth he will be miserable in that which is to come.

Notes on Religion, 1776

August 2

Truth will do well enough if left to shift for herself. She seldom has received much aid from the power of great men to whom she is rarely known and seldom welcome. She has no need of force to procure entrance into the minds of men. Error indeed has often prevailed by the assistance of power or force. Truth is the proper and sufficient antagonist to error.

Ibid.

August 3

I confess that I am not reconciled to the idea of a chief magistrate parading himself through the several states as an object of public gaze and in quest of an applause which to be valuable should be purely voluntary. I had rather acquire silent good will by a faithful discharge of my duties than owe expressions of it to putting myself in the way of receiving them.

Letter to Governor Sullivan, 1807

August 4

Nothing then is unchangeable but the inherent and unalienable rights of men.

Letter to John Cartwright, 1824

August 5

Yours is one of the few lives precious to mankind and for the continuance of which every thinking man is solicitous. Bigots may be an exception. . . . science and honesty are . . . on . . . high ground and you, my dear sir, as their great apostle are on its pinnacle.

Letter to Joseph Priestly, 1801

August 6

The happiest moments of my life have been the few I have passed at home in the bosom of my family. . . . I only say that public employment contributes neither to advantage or happiness. It is but honorable exile from one's family and affairs.

Letter to Frances Willis, 1790*

August 7

In the course of the trusts I have exercised through life with powers of appointment, I can say with truth and with unspeakable comfort that I never did appoint a relation to office . . . because I never saw the case in which someone did not offer or occur better qualified.

Letter to J. C. Cabell, 1824

August 8

Calvin consumed the poor Servetus because he could not find in his Euclid the proposition which has demonstrated that three are one and one is three, nor subscribe to that Calvin notion that magistrates have a right to exterminate all heretics to Calvinist creed.

Letter to William Short, 1820

---

*Jefferson's wife died in 1782.

August 9

[Bring] Plato to the test of reason, take from his sophisms, futilities and incomprehensibilities and what remains? In truth, he is one of the race of sophists who has escaped the oblivion of his brethren first by the elegance of his diction but chiefly by the adoption and incorporation of his whimsies into the body of artificial Christianity. . . . Socrates had reason indeed to complain of the misrepresentations of Plato for, in truth, his dialogues are libels on Socrates.

Letter to John Adams, 1814

August 10

The blasphemy and absurdity of the five points of Calvin and the impossibility of defending them, render their advocates impatient of reasoning, irritable, and prone to denunciation.

Letter to Dr. Cooper, 1822

August 11

The Gothic idea that we are to look backwards instead of forwards for the improvement of the human mind and to recur to the annals of ancestors for what is not perfect in government, in religion and in learning is worthy of those bigots in religion and government by whom it has been recommended and whose purposes it would answer.

Letter to Joseph Priestly, 1800

August 12

Any officer or soldier guilty of mutiny, desertion, disobedience of command, absence from duty or quarters, neglect of guard, or cowardice, shall be punished at the discretion of the court-marshall by degrading, cashiering, drumming out of the army, whipping not exceeding twenty lashes, fine not exceeding two months, or imprisonment not exceeding one month.

From the draft of a bill providing against invasions, 1777

August 13

I cannot give up my guidance to any magistrate because he knows no more of the road to heaven than I do and is less concerned to direct me right than I am to go right. . . . The magistrate has no power but what the people gave. The people have not given him the care of souls because no man has the right to let another prescribe his faith. No man can conform his faith to the dictates of another. The life and essence of religion consists in the internal persuasion or belief of the mind.

Notes on Religion, 1776

August 14

I sincerely believe . . . that banking establishments are more dangerous than standing armies and that the practise of spending money to be paid by posterity, under the name of funding, is but swindling futurity on a large scale.

Letter to John Taylor, 1816

August 15

No man has a right to commit aggression on the equal rights of another. . . . Every man is under the natural duty of contributing to the necessities of the society. . . . The idea is quite unfounded that on entering into society we give up any natural right.

Letter to F. W. Gilmor, 1816

August 16

We have the same object, the success of representative government. Nor are we acting for ourselves alone but for the whole human race. The event of our experiment is to show whether man can be trusted with self-government.

Letter to Governor Hall (not dated)

August 17

Nothing could so completely divest us of our liberty as the establishment of the opinion that the state has a perpetual right to the service of all its members.

Letter to James Monroe, 1782

August 18

The abolition of domestic slavery is the great object of desire in these colonies where it was unhappily introduced. But previous to the enfranchisement of the slaves it is necessary to exclude all further importation from Africa. Yet, our repeated attempts to effect this . . . have . . . been defeated by his majesty's negative, thus preferring the immediate advantages of a few British corsairs to the lasting interests of the American states and to the right of human nature deeply wounded by this infamous practise.

From *A Summary View*, 1774

August 19

I consider the people who constitute a society or nation as the source of all authority in that nation.

From an opinion on French treaties, 1793

August 20

I wish to preserve the line drawn by the Federal Constitution between the general and particular governments as it stands at present and to take every prudent means of preventing either from stepping over it.

Letter to Archibald Stuart, 1791

August 21

If we can keep the vessel of State as steadily in her course another four years, my earthly purposes will be accomplished and I shall be free.

Letter to Elbridge Gerry, 1804

August 22

I cannot be saved by a worship I disbelieve and abhor.

Notes on Religion, 1776

August 23

It is rare that the public sentiment decides universally or unwisely and the individual who differs from it ought to distrust and examine his own opinion.

Letter to William Findley, 1801

August 24

Our country is too large to have all of its affairs directed by a single government. . . . The true theory of our constitution is surely the wisest and the best . . . the States are independent as to everything within themselves and untied as to everything respecting foreign nations. Let the general government be reduced to foreign concerns only.

Letter to Gordon Granger, 1800

August 25

Tobacco is a culture of infinite wretchedness. Those employed in it are in a continual state of exertion beyond the power of nature to support.

Notes on the State of Virginia, 1782

August 26

We are not immortal ourselves, my friend, how can we expect our enjoyments to be so? We have no rose without its thorns, no pleasure without alloy. It is the law of our existence and we must acquiesce.

Letter to Mrs. Maria Conway, 1786

August 27

The new government [of the United States] has ushered itself to the world as honest, masculine, and dignified. It has shown genuine dignity, in my opinion, in exploding adulatory titles. They [titles] are the objects of abject baseness and nourish that degrading vice in the people.

Letter to James Madison, 1789

August 28

Human nature is the same on every side of the Atlantic. . . . The time to guard against corruption and tyranny is before they have gotten hold of us. It is better to keep the wolf out of the fold than to trust to drawing his teeth and talons after he shall have entered.

Notes on the State of Virginia, 1782

August 29

We consider ourselves as bound to honor . . . one general fate with our sister colonies and should hold ourselves base deserters of that union to which we have acceded were we to agree on any measure distinct and apart from them.

From an address to Governor Dunmore of Virginia, 1775

August 30

I do not recollect in all the animal kingdom a single species but man which is eternally and systematically engaged in the destruction of its own species.

Letter to James Madison, 1797

August 31

Be this as it may, in every free and deliberating society, there must . . . be opposite parties and violent dissensions and discords. . . . Perhaps the party division is necessary to induce each to watch over the other.

Letter to John Taylor, 1798

September

September 1

In September, 1782, I lost a cherished companion* of my life in whose affections, unabated on both sides, I had lived the last ten years in unchequered happiness.

Autobiography, 1821

September 2

It is too late in the day . . . to pretend they believe in the Platonic mysticisms that three are one and one is three, and yet that one is not three and the three are not one. . . . But this constitutes the craft, the power and the profits of the priest.

Letter to John Adams, 1813

---

*His wife, age thirty-three.

September 3

If ever you find yourself environed with difficulties and perplexing circumstances . . . follow truth, justice and plain dealing and never fear their leading you out of the labyrinth in the easiest manner possible.

Letter to nephew Peter Carr, 1785

September 4

It is not by consolidation or concentration of powers but by their distribution that good government is effected. Were we directed from Washington when to sow and when to reap we would soon want bread.

Autobiography, 1821

September 5

Our true interest will be best promoted by making all the just claims of our fellow citizens whenever situated our own. . . . No other conduct can attach us together and on this attachment depends our happiness.

Letter to Colonel Monroe, 1786

September 6

I am of the opinion that the Government should firmly maintain this ground; that the Indians have a right to the occupation of their lands independent of the States within whose chartered lands they happen to be. . . . The Government is

determined to exert all its energy for the patronage and protection of the rights of the Indians.

Letter to James Monroe, 1791

September 7

You seem to consider the judges as the ultimate arbiters of all
constitutional questions; a very dangerous doctrine indeed,
and one that would place us under the despotism of an oli-
garchy. Our judges are as honest as other men are and no more
so. They have the same passions for party, for power, and . . .
privilege. . . . I know of no safe depository of the ultimate powers of society but the people themselves and if we think them
not enlightened enough to exercise their control with a whole-
some direction, the remedy is not to take it from them, but to
inform their discretion by education. This is the true corrective
for abuses of constitutional power.

Letter to Mr. Jarvis, 1820

September 8

The most effectual means of being secure against pain is to retire
within ourselves and to suffice for our own happiness. Those who
depend on ourselves are the only pleasures a wise man will count
on. . . . Nothing is ours which another may deprive us of.

Letter to Mrs. Maria Cosway, 1786

September 9

Every political measure will forever have an intimate connec-
tion with the laws of the land. . . . He who knows nothing of

these will always be perplexed and often foiled by adversaries having the advantage of that knowledge over him.

Letter to T. M. Randolph, Jr., 1787

September 10

All facts in causes whether in Chancery, Common, Ecclesiastical, or Marine law shall be tried by a jury upon evidence given viva voce, in open court. . . . All fines or amercements shall be assessed and terms of imprisonment for contempts and misdemeanors shall be fixed by a jury.

From a proposed constitution for Virginia, 1776

September 11

When we get piled upon one another in large cities, as in Europe, we shall be corrupt as in Europe and go to eating one another as they do there.

Letter to James Madison, 1787

September 12

I had rather be shut up in a very modest cottage with my books, my family and a few old friends . . . than to occupy the most splendid post which any human power can give.

Letter to A. Donald, 1788

September 13

I see Kosciusko often and with great pleasure mixed with com-miseration. He is as pure a son of liberty as I have ever known and of that liberty which is to go to all and not to the few or the rich alone.

Letter to Horatius Gates, 1798

September 14

I suppose this ground to be self-evident, that the earth belongs in usufruct to the living, the dead have neither power nor rights over it.

Letter to James Madison, 1789

September 15

We have already given, in example, one effectual check to the dog of war by transferring the power of declaring war from the executive to the legislative body, from those who are to spend to those who are to pay.

Ibid.

September 16

Were her system [the Duchesse de La Rochefoucault] of ethics and of government the system of every one, we should have no occasion for government at all.

Letter to Duke de La Rochefoucault, 1790

September 17

A host of writers have risen in favor of [Tom] Paine and prove that in this quarter, at least, the spirit of republicanism is sound.

Letter to Colonel Monroe, 1791

September 18

I never did in my life, either by myself or by any other, have a sentence of mine inserted in a newspaper without putting my name to it; and I believe I never shall.

Letter to John Adams, 1791

September 19

We certainly cannot deny to other nations that principle whereon our government is founded—that every nation has a right to govern itself internally under what form it pleases and to change these forms at its own will.

Letter to Mr. Pickney, 1792

September 20

You probably do not know Mr. Madison personally, or at least as intimately as I do. I have known him from 1779, . . . and from three and thirty years trial I can say conscientiously that I do not know in the world a man of purer integrity, more dispassionate, disinterested and devoted to genuine republicanism, nor could I . . . point out an abler head.

Letter to T. C. Florey, 1812

September 21

When a man whose life has been marked by its candor has given a later opinion contrary to a former one, it is probably the result of further inquiry, reflection and conviction.

Letter to Peregrine Fitzhugh, 1798

September 22

I do not indeed wish to see any nation have a form of government forced on them but if it is to be done, I should rejoice at it being a free one.

Ibid.

September 23

To our reproach it must be said that for a century and a half we have had under our eyes the races of black and of red men, [but] they have never yet been viewed by us as subjects of natural history.

Notes on the State of Virginia, 1782

September 24

Rights and powers can only belong to persons, not to things, not to mere matter, unendowed with will. The dead are not even things. The particles of matter which composed their bodies, make part now of the bodies of other animals, vegetables or minerals of a thousand forms.

Letter to John Cartwright, 1824

September 25

I am for a government rigorously frugal and simple, applying all possible savings of the public revenue to the discharge of the national debt . . . not for the multiplication of officers and salaries merely to make partisans and for increasing . . . the public debt on the principle of its being a public blessing.

Letter to Elbridge Gerry, 1789

September 26

The first object of my heart is my own country. In that is embarked my family, my fortune and my own existence. I have not one farthing of interest, nor one fibre of attachment out of it, nor a single motive of preference of any one nation to another but in proportion as they are more or less friendly to us.

Ibid.

September 27

The influence over government must be shared by all the people. If every individual who composes their mass participates of the ultimate authority, the government will be safe . . . because corrupting the whole mass will exceed any private resources of wealth and public ones cannot be provided but by levies on the whole people.

Notes on the State of Virginia, 1782

September 28

I hope that the French revolution will issue happily. I feel that the permanence of our own leans in some degree on that, and that failure there would be a powerful argument to prove a failure here.

Letter to Edward Rutledge, 1791

September 29

I will never by any word or act bow to the shrine of intolerance, or admit a right of inquiry into the religious opinions of others.

Letter to Edward Dowse, 1803

September 30

The Legislature should never show itself in a matter with a foreign nation, but where the case is very serious and they mean to commit the nation in its issue.

Letter to James Madison, 1791

October

October 1

I may err in my measures but never shall deflect from the intention to fortify public liberty by every possible means and to put it out of the power of the few to riot on the labors of the many.

Letter to Judge Tyler, 1804

October 2

I should unwillingly be the person who, disregarding the sound precedent set by an illustrious predecessor, should furnish the first example of prolongation beyond the second term of office.

Letter to the General Assembly of North Carolina, 1808

October 3

My usage is to make the best appointment my information and judgement enable me to do and then fold myself up in the

105

mantle of conscience and abide unmoved by the peltings of the storm.

Letter to Benjamin Rush, 1808

October 4

Reading, reflection and time have convinced me that the interests of society require the observation of those moral precepts only in which all religions agree. . . . We should not intermeddle with the particular dogmas . . . which are totally unconnected with morality.

Letter to James Fishback, 1809

October 5

The principles of our constitution are wisely opposed to all perpetuations of power and to every practise which may lead to hereditary establishments.

Letter to Messrs. Bloodgood and Hammond, 1809

October 6

A second class at the head of which is our quondam colleague [Hamilton] are ardent for the introduction of monarchy, eager for armies, making more noise for a great naval establishment than better patriots who wish it on a national scale only, commensurate to our wants and our means. This class ought to be tolerated but not trusted.

Letter to Henry Knox, 1801

October 7

Every one, certainly, must form his judgement on the evidence available to himself. . . . I have no more doubt of the integrity of your convictions than I have of my own.

Letter to Colonel William Duane, 1811

October 8

For us to attempt, by war, to reform all Europe and bring them back to principles of morality and a respect for the equal rights of nations, would show us to be only maniacs of another character. We should, indeed, have the merit of good intentions as well as the folly of the hero of La Mancha.

Letter to Mr. Wirt, 1811

October 9

I should say, put down all banks, admit none but a metallic circulation that will take its proper level with the like circulation in other countries. . . . Then our manufacturers may work in fair competition with those of other countries.

Letter to Mr. Pinckney, 1820

October 10

I know of nothing which can so severely try the heart and spirit of man, and especially the men of science, as the necessity of acquiescence under the abominations of an unprincipled tyrant.

Letter to Dr. Morrell, 1813

October 11

We lay it down as a fundamental that laws to be just must give a reciprocation of right. . . . Without this they are mere arbitrary rules of conduct founded in force and not in conscience.

Notes on the State of Virginia, 1782

October 12

No writer has exceeded Paine in ease and familiarity of style, in perspicuity of expression, happiness of elucidation and in simple unassuming language.

Letter to Frances Eppes, 1821

October 13

May it [the fiftieth anniversary of the Declaration of Independence] be to the world the . . . signal of arousing men to burst the chains under which monkish ignorance and superstition had persuaded them to bind themselves and to assume the blessings of liberty and self-government.

Letter to Mr. Weightman, 1826*

October 14

I have thought it my duty . . . that in selecting persons for the management of their affairs, I am influenced by neither personal nor family interests and especially that the field of public office will not be perverted by me into a family property.

Letter to Horatio Turpin, 1807

---

*Jefferson died July 4, 1826.

October 15

It is between fifty and sixty years since I read it [Revelation] and then I considered it to be the ravings of a maniac, no more worthy nor capable of explanation than the incoherence of our own nightly dreams. . . . What has no meaning admits no explanation.

Letter to General Alexander Smith, 1825

October 16

No person shall be capable of acting in any office, civil or military, who shall have given any bribe to obtain such office.

From a proposed constitution for Virginia, 1776

October 17

But is an enemy so execrable that though in captivity his wishes and comforts are to be entirely disregarded and even crossed? I think not. It is for the benefit of mankind to mitigate the horrors of war as much as possible.

Letter to Patrick Henry, 1779

October 18

We are all doubtless bound to contribute a certain portion of our income to the support of charitable and other useful public institutions. But it is part of our duty also to apply our contributions in the most effectual way we can to secure this object.

Letter to Samuel Kercheval, 1810

October 19

I am astonished at some people's considering a kingly government as a refuge. . . . If all the evils which can arise among us
from the Republican form of our government from this day to
the day of judgment could be put into a scale against what this
country suffers from its monarchial form in a week, or England
in a month, the latter would preponderate.

Letter to Benjamin Hawkings, written from Paris, 1787

October 20

Of all the doctrines which have ever been broached by the Federal government the novel one of the common law being in
force and cognizable as an existing law in their courts is, to me,
the most formidable.

Letter to Edmund Randolph, 1799

October 21

I like the power given to the legislature to levy taxes and for
that reason solely approve of the greater House being chosen
by the people directly. For though I think a House chosen by
them will be very illy qualified to legislate for the Union, for
foreign nations etc., yet this evil does not weigh against the
good of preserving inviolate the fundamental principle that the
people are not to be taxed but by representatives chosen immediately by themselves.

Letter to James Madison, 1787

October 22

I join those in opinion who think a Bill of Rights necessary. I apprehended too that the total abandonment of the principle of rotation in the office of President and Senator will end in abuse. . . . We can surely boast of having set the world a beautiful example of a government reformed by reason alone [and] without bloodshed.

Letter to Edward Rutledge, 1788

October 23

I give one answer to all the theorists. . . . They all suppose the earth a created existence; they must suppose a Creator then and that he possessed the power and wisdom to a great degree. As he intended the earth for the habitation of animals and vegetables, is it reasonable to suppose he made two jobs of the creation? That he first made a chaotic lump and set it in motion, and then, when it had done this, he stepped in a second time to create the animals and plants which were to inhabit it? . . . We may as well suppose he created the earth at once nearly in the state we see it.

Letter to Charles Thompson, 1786

October 24

I own it to be my opinion that good will arise from the destruction of our credit. I see nothing else which can restrain our disposition to luxury and the loss of these manners which can preserve Republican government. As it is impossible to prevent credit, the best way to cure its ill effects [is] by giving instantaneous recovery to the creditor; this would be reducing purchases on credit to purchases for ready money.

Letter to A. Stuart, 1786

October 25

What is true of every member of the society individually is true of them all collectively, since the rights of the whole can be no more than the sum of the rights of the individuals. . . . No generation can contract debts greater than may be paid during the course of its own existence.

Letter to James Madison, 1789

October 26

A member of society committing an inferior injury, does not wholly forfeit the protection of his fellow citizens. . . . After suffering a punishment in proportion to his offence [he] is entitled to their protection from all greater pain. . . . It becomes the duty of the Legislature to arrange in a proper scale the crimes . . . and to adjust thereto a corresponding gradation of punishment.

From a Bill Relating to Crimes and Punishments, 1779

October 27

A public institution can only supply those sciences which, though rarely called for, are yet necessary to complete the circle, all the parts of which contribute to the improvement of the country, and some of them to its preservation. . . . The present consideration of a national establishment for education . . . is

. . . proper. . . . I suppose an amendment to the Constitution, by consent of the states, necessary, because the objects now recommended are not among those enumerated in the Constitution and to which it permits public moneys to be applied.

Sixth Annual Message to Congress, 1806

October 28

I am much pleased to see that you have taken up the subject of the duty on imported books. I hope a crusade will be kept up against it until those in power shall become sensible of this stain on our legislation and shall wipe it from their code.

Letter to Jared Sparks, 1824

October 29

As you say of yourself, I too am an Epicurean. I consider the genuine . . . doctrines of Epicurus as containing everything rational in moral philosophy. . . . Epictetus and Epicurus give laws for governing ourselves.

Letter to William Short, 1819

October 30

I had rather ask an enlargement of power from the nation, where it is found necessary, than to assume it by a construction which would make our powers boundless. Our peculiar security is in possession of a written Constitution. Let us not make it a blank paper by construction. . . . Let us go on then perfecting it by adding, by way of amendment . . . those powers which time and trial show are still wanting. . . . I think it important

... to set an example against broad construction by appealing for new power to the people. If, however, our friends shall think differently, certainly I shall acquiesce with satisfaction, confiding that the good sense of our country will correct the evil of construction when it shall produce ill effects.

Letter to W. C. Nicholas, 1803

October 31

Give about two hours every day to exercise. . . . Health must not be sacrificed to learning. A strong body makes the mind strong. . . . Walking is the best possible exercise. Habituate yourself to walk very far. . . . There is no habit you will value so much as that of walking far without fatigue. . . . A little walk of half an hour in the morning . . . shakes off sleep and produces other good effects in the animal economy.

Letter to Peter Cartwright, 1785

November

November 1

I believe with you that morality, compassion, generosity are innate elements of the human constitution. . . . A right to property is founded in our natural wants, in the means by which we are endowed to satisfy those wants, and the right to acquire by those means without violating the similar rights of other sensible beings. . . . No one has the right to obstruct another.

Letter to Dupont de Nemours, 1816

November 2

Whenever Bonaparte meddled we have seen nothing but fragments of the old Roman government stuck on to materials with which they can form no cohesion. We see the bigotry of an Italian to the ancient splendor of his country but nothing that speaks the luminous view of the organization of a rational government.

Letter to Thomas Mann Randolph, 1800

115

November 3

I consider the fortunes of our republic as depending in an imminent degree on the extinguishment of the public debt. . . . If the debt should once more be swelled to a formidable size, its entire discharge will be despaired of, and we shall be committed to the English career of debt, corruption and rottenness, closing with revolution. The discharge of the debt, therefore, is vital to the destinies of our government.

Letter to Albert Gallatin, 1809

November 4

The earth is given a common stock for man to live on. . . . It is too soon yet in our country to say that every man who cannot find employment but who can find uncultivated land shall be at liberty to cultivate it, paying a wholesale rent. But it is not too soon to provide by every possible means that as few as possible shall be without a little portion of land. The small landholders are the most precious part of the State.

Letter to Reverend James Madison, 1795

November 5

In the constitution of Spain . . . was a principle entirely new to me. . . . No person . . . should ever acquire the rights of citizenship until he could read and write. It is impossible to sufficiently establish the wisdom of that principle. . . . Enlighten the people generally and tyranny and oppression will vanish.

Letter to Dupont de Nemours, 1816

November 6

When a nation imposes high duties on our productions or pro-hibits them altogether, it may be proper for us to do the same by theirs . . . excluding those productions which they bring here in competition with our own of the same kind.

From a Report on the Commerce
of the United States, 1793

November 7

A Constitution has been acquired which, though neither of us thinks perfect, yet both consider as competent to render our fellow citizens the happiest and the securest upon whom the sun has ever shone. . . . We have delivered over to our succes-sors in life who will be able to take care of it and themselves.

Letter to John Adams, 1813

November 8

Another means of silently lessening the inequality of property is to exempt all from taxation below a certain point and to tax the higher portions of property in a geometrical progression as they rise.

Letter to Reverend James Madison, 1795

November 9

I hope we shall take the warning from the example of England and crush in its birth the aristocracy of our moneyed corpora-

tions which dare already to challenge our government to trial
and bid defiance to the laws of our country.

Letter to George Logan, 1816

November 10

Reason and nature clearly pronounce that the neutral is to go
in the enjoyment of its rights, that its commerce remains free,
not subject to the jurisdiction of another.

Letter to the Minister of France, 1801

November 11

A right of free correspondence between citizen and citizen on
their joint interests, whether public or private . . . is a natural
right. It is not the gift of any municipal law either of England
or Virginia or the Congress. . . . In common with all other natural rights [it] is one of the objects for protection of which
society is formed and municipal laws are established.

Letter to James Monroe, 1797

November 12

"Never to borrow a dollar without laying a tax in the same
instant for paying the interest annually and the principle
within a given term, and to consider that tax as pledged to the
creditors on the public faith." On such a pledge as this, sacredly
observed, a government may always command . . . all the lend-
able money of its citizens.

Letter to J. W. Eppes, 1813

November 13

Above all things I hope the education of the common people will be attended to. . . . On their good sense we may rely with the most security for the preservation of a due degree of liberty.

Letter to James Madison, 1787

November 14

Friendship is precious, not only in the shade but in the sunshine of life. . . . Thanks to a benevolent arrangement of things, the greater part of life is sunshine. . . . Believe me, then, my friend that that is a miserable arithmetic which could estimate friendship at nothing.

Letter to Mrs. Maria Cosway, 1786

November 15

Open your breast, sire, to liberal and expanded thought. Let not the name of George the Third be a blot in the page of history. You have no Minister for American affairs. . . . It behooves you, therefore to think and act for yourself and the people. . . . No longer persevere in sacrificing the rights of one part of the empire to the inordinate desires of another but deal out to all, equal and impartial right.

A *Summary View*, 1774

November 16

I do not at all wonder at the condition in which the finances of the United States are found. Hamilton's object . . . was to throw them into forms which should be utterly undecipherable. If Mr. Gallitan [Secretary of the Treasury appointed by Jefferson] would undertake to reduce this chaos to order, present us with a clear view of our finances and put them in a form as simple as they will admit, he will merit immortal honor. The accounts of the United States ought to be and may be made as simple as those of a common farmer and capable of being understood by common farmers.

Letter to James Madison, 1796

November 17

To oppose his [George III's] arms we also have taken up arms. We should be wanting to ourselves, we should be perfidious to posterity, we should be unworthy that ancestry from which we derive our descent, should we submit with folded arms to military butchery and depredation to gratify the lordly ambition or to sate the avarice of a British ministry.

From a Declaration Submitted to Congress Declaring the Reasons Why Americans Had Taken Up Arms, 1775

November 18

We had reposed great confidence in that provision of the constitution which requires two-thirds of the Legislature to declare war. Yet it may be entirely eluded by a majority's taking such measures as will bring on war.

Letter to James Monroe, 1798

November 19

It is fortunate that our first Executive Magistrate [President George Washington] is purely and zealously Republican. We cannot expect all his successors to be so and therefore should avail ourselves the present day to establish principles and examples which may fence us against heresies preached now to be practised hereafter.

Letter to Harry Innes, 1791

November 20

It may be mentioned as proof both of the lenity of our government that though the war has now raged near seven years, not a single execution for treason has taken place.

Notes on the State of Virginia, 1782

November 21

We are ruined, Sir, if we do not overrule the principle that, "the more we owe the more prosperous we shall be." That a public debt furnishes the means of our enterprise and that ours should be paid off, we should incur another by any means.

Letter to James Madison, 1791

November 22

The denouement [referring to the acquisition of Louisiana] has been happy. . . . I look to the duplication of area for extending government so free and economical as ours as a great achievement to the mass of happiness that is to ensue.

Letter to Dr. Joseph Priestly, 1804

November 23

It is hoped that by a due poise and partition of powers between the general [federal] and particular [state]) governments, we may have found the secret of extending the benign blessings of republicanism over still greater tracts than we possess.

Letter to James Sullivan, 1791

November 24

A lively and lasting sense of filial duty is more effectually impressed on the mind of a son or daughter by reading King Lear than by all the dry volumes of ethics and divinity that ever were written.

Letter to Robert Skipworth, 1771

November 25

As far as my good will may go . . . I shall adhere to my government, executive and legislative, and, as long as they are Republican, I shall go with their measures, whether I think them right or wrong because I know they are honest . . . and better informed than I.

Letter to William Duane, 1811

November 26

I hold it to be one of the distinguishing excellencies of election over hereditary succession that the talents nature has provided in sufficient proportion should be selected by the society for the government of their affairs rather than this should be transmitted through the loins of knaves and fools passing from the debauches of the table to those of the bed.

Letter to George Washington, 1792

November 27

Like my friend the doctor, I have lived temperately, eating little animal food and that not as an aliment so much as a condiment for the vegetables which constitute my principle diet. I double, however, the doctor's glass and a half of wine and even treble it with a friend but halve its effects by drinking the weak wines only. The ardent wines I cannot drink nor do I use ardent spirits in any form. . . . I have not lost a tooth by age. . . . Whether I retire to bed early or late, I rise with the sun.

Letter to Dr. Vine Utley, 1819*

November 28

Let us then, fellow-citizens, unite with one heart and one mind. Let us restore to social intercourse that harmony and affection without which liberty and even life itself are but dreary things. And let us reflect that having banished from our land that religious intolerance under which mankind so long bled and suffered, we have gained little, if we countenance a

---

*Jefferson was then seventy-six.

political intolerance as despotic, as wicked and capable of bitter and bloody persecutions.

First Inaugural Address, 1801

November 29

Those who have had and may yet have occasion to ask great favors, should never ask small ones.

Letter to Lafayette, 1786

November 30

The death of our friend Mazzei's wife has given him three-quarters of the globe elbow room, which he had ceded to her, on condition that she would leave him quiet in the fourth. Their partition of the next world will be more difficult, if it be divided only into two parts, according to the Protestant faith.

Letter to Mr. Bellini, 1788

December

December 1

As the character of the Prince of Wales is becoming interesting, I have endeavored to learn what it really is. . . . He has not a single element of mathematics or moral philosophy or any other science on earth. . . . He has not a single idea of justice, morality, religion or the rights of men or any anxiety for the opinion of the world. . . . He probably would not be hurt if he was to lose his throne provided he could be assured of having always his meat, horses and women.

Letter to John Jay, 1789

December 2

Canons of Conduct
1. Never put off for tomorrow what you can do today.
2. Never trouble another for what you can do for yourself.
3. Never spend money before you have it.
4. Never buy what you do not want because it is cheap. . . .

5. Pride costs us more than hunger, thirst and cold.

6. We never repent of having eaten too little.

7. Nothing is troublesome that we do willingly.

8. How much pain cost us the evils which have never happened.

9. Take things always by their smooth handle.

10. When angry count ten before you speak; if very angry an hundred.

Letter to Thomas Jefferson Smith, 1825

December 3

When we consider that this government is charged with the external and mutual relations only of these States (that the States themselves have the principal care of persons, our property and our reputations) . . . we may well doubt whether our organization is not too complicated, too expensive [and] whether offices and officers have not multiplied unnecessarily and sometimes injuriously to the service they were meant to promote. . . . I have begun the reduction of what was deemed necessary. The expenses of the diplomatic agency have been considerably diminished. The inspectors of internal revenue who were found to obstruct accountability of the institution have been discontinued. Several agencies created by executive authority . . . have been suppressed. . . .

First Annual Message to Congress, 1801

December 4

I observe a bill is now pending in Parliament for the relief of Anti-Trinitarians. It is too late in the day for men of sincerity to pretend they believe in the Platonic mysticisms, that three are one, and one is three; and yet that one is not three, and the three are not one.

Letter to John Adams, 1813

December 5

[N]o man is more ardently intent to see the public debt soon and sacredly paid off than I am. This exactly marks the difference between Colonel Hamilton's views and mine, that I would wish the debt to be paid tomorrow; he wishes it never to be paid off but always a thing wherewith to corrupt and man-age the legislature.

Letter to President George Washington, 1792

December 6

Truth can stand by itself. Subject opinion to coercion: whom will you make the inquisitors? Fallible men; men governed by bad passions, by prvate as well as public reasons. And why subject it to coercion? To produce uniformity. But is uniformity of opinion desirable?

Notes on the State of Virginia, 1782

December 7

Even error in the highest court is one of these inconveniences flowing from the imperfections of our faculties, to which every society must submit; because there must be somewhere a last resort wherein contestations may end. Multiply revisal as you please, their number will be finite and they must finish in the hands of fallible men as judges.

Letter to the British Minister, 1792

December 8

When the representative body have lost the confidence of their constituents, when they have notoriously made sale of their most valuable rights, when they have assumed . . . powers which the people never put in their hands . . . [this] calls for an exercise of the power of dissolution.

A Summary View, 1774

December 9

We have chanced to live in an age which will probably be distinguished in history for its experiments in government on a larger scale than has yet taken place. But we shall not live to see the result. The grosser absurdities such as hereditary magistrates, we shall see exploded in our day.

Letter to M. D'Ivernois, 1795

December 10

Property wrongfully taken from a friend on a high sea is not thereby transferred to the captor. In whatever hands it is found it remains the property of those from whom it was taken.

To Secretary of State James Madison, 1801

December 11

Every man and every body of men has the right of self-government. They receive it with their being from the hand of nature.

> From an opinion on whether the President
> should veto a bill that would move the seat
> of government to the Potomac, 1790

December 12

I believe we may lessen the danger of buying and selling votes by making the number of voters too great for any means of purchase. I may further say that I have not observed men's honesty to increase with their riches.

> Letter to Jeremiah Moore, 1800

December 13

The present desire of America is to produce rapid population by as great an importation of foreigners as possible. But is this founded on good policy? . . . Are there no inconveniences to be thrown on the scale against this advantage?

> *Notes on the State of Virginia*, 1782

December 14

We shall never give up our Union, the last anchor of our hope and that alone which is to prevent this heavenly country from becoming an arena of gladiators.

> Letter to Elbridge Gerry, 1797

December 15

Nor was the unity of the Supreme Being ousted from Christianity by the force of reason but by the sword of civil government, wielded at the will of the fanatic Athanasius. The hocus-pocus phantasm of a God like another Cerebus with one body and three heads, had its birth and growth in the blood of thousands and thousands of martyrs.

Letter to James Smith, 1822

December 16

I think I knew General Washington intimately and thoroughly. ... The strongest feature of his character was prudence.... His integrity was most pure; his justice the most inflexible I have ever known.... He was indeed, in every sense of the word a wise, a good, a great man.

Written shortly after Washington's death, 1799

December 17

I have often wished we could have a philosophical society or academy so organized as that while the central academy should be at the seat of government, its members dispersed over the State should constitute filiated academies in each State.... The great societies now existing might incorporate themselves in this way with a National one.

Letter to Joel Barlow, 1805

December 18

A letter from you, my respected friend, after three and twenty years of separation, has given me a pleasure I cannot express. It recalls to my mind the anxious days we then passed in struggling for mankind. Your principles have been tested in the crucible of time and have come out pure. You have proved that it was monarchy and not just British monarchy you opposed.

Letter to Samuel Adams, 1800

December 19

Deeply practised in the school of affliction, the human heart knows no joy which I have not lost, no sorrow of which I have not drunk! Fortune can present no grief of unknown form to me. Who then can so softly bind up the wound of another as he who has felt the same wound himself.

Letter to Mrs. Maria Cosway, 1786

December 20

In truth, the ultimate point of rest and happiness for them [the Indians] is to let our settlements and theirs meet and blend together, to intermix and become one people, incorporating themselves with us as citizens of the United States. . . . This is what the natural progress of things will . . . bring on and it will be better to promote it than retard it.

Letter to Benjamin Hawkins, 1803

December 21

A modern bishop to be moulded into a primitive one must be elected by the people, undiocesed, unreverenced, unlorded.

Notes on Religion, 1776

December 22

Our civil rights have no dependence on our religious opinions any more than on our opinions in physics or geometry. . . . The proscribing of any citizen as unworthy of the public confidence . . . unless he profess or renounce this or that religious opinion, is depriving him judicially of those privileges and advantages to which, in common with his fellow citizens, he has a natural right.

Bill for Establishing Religious Freedom, 1779

December 23

Be you, my dear, the link of love, union and peace for the whole family. The world will give you more credit for it, in proportion to the difficulty of the task.

An appeal to his daughter Martha, 1790

December 24

Determined as we are to avoid, if possible, wasting the energies of our people in war and destruction, we shall avoid implicating ourselves with the powers of Europe even in support of the principles we mean to pursue.

Letter to Thomas Paine, 1801

December 25

That the purest system of morals ever before preached to man has been adulterated, sophisticated by artificial constructions into a mere contrivance to filch wealth and power to themselves [the clergy]; that rational men not being able to swallow their impious heresies . . . they raise the hue and cry of infidelity which they themselves are the greatest obstacles to the advancement of the real doctrines of Jesus and do, in fact, constitute the real Anti-Christ.

Letter to Samuel Kercheval, 1810

December 26

It is however, an evil for which there is no remedy, our liberty depends on the freedom of the press, and that cannot be limited.

Letter to Dr. J. Currie, 1786

December 27

Let the gloomy monk, sequestered from the world, seek unsocial pleasures in the bottom of his cell. Let the sublimated philosopher grasp visionary happiness while pursuing phantoms dressed in the garb of truth. Their supreme wisdom is supreme folly. Had they ever felt the solid pleasure of one generous spasm of the heart, they would exchange it for all the frigid speculations of their lives.

Letter to Mrs. Maria Cosway, 1786

December 28

I contemplate with sovereign reverence that act of the whole American people which declared that their legislature should make no law respecting an establishment of religion, or prohibit the free exercise thereof, thus building a wall of separation between church and state.

To the Baptists of Danbury, Connecticut, 1802*

December 29

On the dogmas of religion . . . all mankind . . . have been quarreling, fighting, burning and torturing one another, for abstractions unintelligible to themselves and all others, and absolutely beyond the comprehension of the human mind.

To Mr. Carey, 1816, quoted by S. Padover

December 30

The boisterous sea of liberty is never without a wave. Had there never been a commentator there never would have been an infidel.

Letter to Mrs. Harrison Smith, 1816

December 31

I have sometimes asked myself whether my country is the better for my having lived at all. I do not know that it is.

Probably written in 1800

---

*It was President Jefferson who, while in office, made this statement!

Index